SOCCER
TECHNIQUES.

A GUIDE FOR TEACHERS AND COACHES.

TREVOR
SPINDLER

First printed 1993 by The City Print Buying Centre Ltd., London E8.4DG.

© 1993 Trevor Spindler.

ISBN 0 9520030 0 7

A CIP catalogue record for this book is available from the British Library.

Illustrations by Debbie Hart.

Photographs by Tom Harris and Associated Sports Photography, Leicester.

Cover photograph: Gary Lineker (England) scores the equalizing goal against West Germany in the 1990 World Cup semi-final.

Printed and bound in Great Britain by The City Print Buying Centre Ltd., London E8.4DG.

CONTENTS

Foreword   4

Introduction   5

1. THE BASICS OF COACHING   7

2. PASSING   15

3. GAINING TIME ON THE BALL   41

4. SHOOTING   56

5. HEADING   69

6. DEFENDING   79

7. GOALKEEPING   91

Conclusion   110

Index   111

Foreword

Coaching has an important part to play in ensuring players reach their potential at whatever level , from local football to full international. Sound technique is an essential aspect of this development and this book provides valuable guidance on how to ensure players develop good technique through correct practice.

Mark Wright

(Liverpool and England)

Acknowledgements

I would like to thank Mark Wright (Liverpool and England) and Eddie Niedzwiecki (Chelsea and Wales) for their contributions to the photographs in this book.

I would also like to thank the many coaches from whom, over the years by watching and listening, I have learned so much.

INTRODUCTION.

It has often been said that Soccer is a simple game, but it is more correct to say that good players make it look simple. Soccer is in fact far from simple, as it consists of so many different elements, for example, passing, control, dribbling, turning, shooting, heading and goalkeeping.

In a game where all the 22 players on the field are free to move wherever and whenever they wish, no two situations which occur will be absolutely identical, but they may well be similar. A good player is able to:

1) Accurately recognise or predict a situation in a game.
2) Make a correct decision about what to do.
3) Perform the appropriate technique to a high level.

No player will do all of these things, all of the time, but these are the qualities of a skilful player and the better the player, the more often he will do them.

Unfortunately, unless a player has good technical ability, that is, the capacity to perform a technique well, the gifts he has in the other two areas will count for little. For this reason, it is vital that young players are given maximum opportunity to develop good technique and older players to maintain or improve the level of technique they already have. This will be best achieved through continued and correct practice which teachers and coaches should provide. That is not to say players should be allowed to practise only technique - once good basic technique is shown, practice situations should become progressively more difficult, involving both opponents and team-mates and culminating in realistic practice matches. Such instances give the experience necessary for developing the essential ability to recognise situations and make appropriate decisions based on them, whilst retaining a high level of technique.

All of the practices shown in this book follow this pattern, but deal only with the coaching of techniques and not the tactics, strategies and systems of play within which those techniques might be used. This book is a valuable guide for both teachers and managers involved in coaching players of all ages. The practices shown have been tried and tested, although there are literally thousands of others which might be used. Coaches should have the individuality and initiative to devise their own practices and also to learn from seeing others coach.

In all of the practices the players are referred to as 'he', but this is merely for the sake of simplicity and the players concerned could be just as easily 'she.' It is recommended that practice should start with the player's preferred foot, but as early as possible the opportunity should be provided to use the weaker foot. The best players are almost equally adept at using either foot on demand during match situations and this has come as a result of continuous and intensive practice. All of the practices given are progressive in nature, that is they gradually become more difficult, either by changing the nature of the service, the size of the area or by introducing more opposition.

All the diagrams in this book use the symbols:

←——————— = PATH OF PLAYER.

←- - - - - - = PATH OF BALL.

1. THE BASICS OF COACHING.

Coaching soccer involves three essential aspects - organisation, observation and communication. If you can do these three things well you are a long way towards being an effective coach.

Coaching will initially take place in an individual or small group situation, but should later be part of small-sided games. The requirements of each from a coaching point of view are somewhat different.

INDIVIDUAL AND SMALL GROUP PRACTICES.

1. ORGANISATION.

When a practice is organised correctly this will maximise the players' learning. It has been suggested that if the organisation is correct, players may learn even without being coached. Clearly, this aspect of coaching is therefore important.

(A) PRE-SESSION ORGANISATION.

(i) Know the subject or topic.

Within each technique under "what to coach" are given the main coaching points or key factors. These are the parts which are essential for the correct performance of the whole technique and should be dealt with preferably one at a time to avoid confusion. This is rather like a young child learning individual letters before putting them together to make a word. The order in which the key factors are introduced can also be important and some sort of logical order is needed. Before beginning a session, the coach should be familiar with the key factors for the technique or topic which is being covered.

(ii) Know the players.

Whenever possible the age and ability of the players should be taken into account when planning a session. Even the best practice is reduced in value if the players find it too easy or too difficult. It is vital to match the topic to the players, rather than the other way round.

(iii) Plan the Session.

This means deciding how the practice will actually operate, for example the number of players involved and the size and location of the practice area. For a practice to be realistic there should be either team-mates or opponents, or both and the number of players should be appropriate to the area being used, or the players will find the practice either too easy or too difficult. The chosen practices should also be "progressive". This means that they should start fairly simply, but get gradually more difficult, because players are unlikely to be able to perform a technique correctly in a difficult situation, if they cannot perform it in a simple one.

(iv) Prepare the Equipment.

Ensure that all the necessary equipment is available and ready - footballs, training bibs, cones, goals, coaching grids or pitch area. These needs will vary dependant on the topic being coached. Training bibs are useful during all opposed practices and are essential for small-sided games. Practice areas can be marked out with cones, although coaching grids are ideal. A coaching grid is an area divided up into boxes of about 10 yards square, which are used for small group practices or small-sided games. (See diagram below.) The lines help to contain and restrict the players and prevent them from wandering. In the absence of grids, the lines of a pitch, gym or sports hall can be used to mark out small areas.

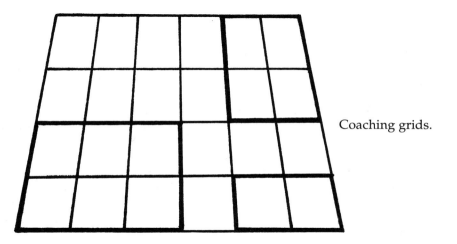

Coaching grids.

(B) ORGANISATION DURING THE SESSION.

(i) Get the Players Working.

Players learn by doing. There is little point in long explanations which may only serve to confuse. Get them working as quickly as possible, perhaps after a brief instruction and walk-through demonstration of how a practice works. Although no specific warm-up or stretching exercises are mentioned in this book, it is essential that the players have done these prior to starting any practice which involves strenuous activity, otherwise injuries may occur.

(ii) Check the Start of the Practice.

Check that the players are in the correct positions, especially at the beginning of the practice. Check that the practice is starting according to instructions.

(iii) Check the Quality of Service.

The importance of this factor cannot be overstressed as many practices are dependant upon the ball being accurately and correctly served. Check that this is so, whether from the hands or feet. If a kicked service is poor, revert to a thrown one. No player can practice any technique if the ball is not placed in the correct position for that technique.

Summary: The organisation should be such that a player is encouraged to learn, even without being coached.

2. OBSERVATION.

Observation is arguably the most difficult aspect of coaching. If you are unable to determine exactly what a player is doing wrong, it is extremely unlikely that you will be able to tell him how to put it right.

(i)   The best place from which the coach should observe is on the outside of the group. This will ensure that all the players are in view and also that he does not inadvertently get in the players' way. When actually coaching he may, of course, move wherever he needs.

(ii) The coach's attention may be directed at two levels - the group and the individual. The first approach is where the general level of performance of the group is observed. If a general fault is seen, the group is stopped for a coaching point or key factor to be made to them all. Practice then continues and the group is further observed to see whether the fault still exists. If it does, a more careful and detailed explanation may be necessary. Where the fault is now limited to a few individuals, the second level of observation is required - that of diagnosing individual faults. In this instance the rest of the   group may continue practising, whilst individual coaching is given as required.

(iii) With regard to technique practices, the key factor approach (see 1(i) above) not only helps the players, but also the coach. It will help him to focus his attention on a specific aspect of a technique and it should therefore be easier to determine whether a fault exists and if so, how to correct it.

(iv) One aspect of a coach's observation must be in deciding when the players are ready to progress, as there is no point in continuing to practise in a situation which has already been mastered. The greatest difficulty comes when some players are ready to progress and others are not. One solution is to impose conditions on some players to make the practice more difficult, for example, 'use the weaker foot' or change the starting positions of the players.

(v) Even so, in some instances, the coach may observe that the technique may be beyond the capabilities of the individual in the situation created. If so, the practice must be made easier. This is usually done by reducing or eliminating opposition, or making the service easier, or changing the size of the practice area. It is essential that when planning coaching sessions the age and ability of the players is taken into account.

(vi) If there is a psychological barrier such as fear, inhibiting performance, then even maximum enthusiasm from the coach may not be successful. A common example of this is heading or tackling with young players.

Summary: In short, the coach's job is to observe at what level to coach the group generally and the individuals within it specifically.

3. COMMUNICATION.

No matter how good a coach's organisation and how perceptive his observation, the final evaluation of his effectiveness will be based on the way he communicates information to the players. This 'feedback' is essential if players are to improve their technique and may be presented in two basic ways -

(a)   Verbal instruction.
(b)   Demonstration.

Invariably, a combination of the two is used.

(A)   VERBAL INSTRUCTION.

Verbal instruction is the most common method of communication used by coaches. The biggest pitfall in its use, is its over-use! It is necessary both for group and individual coaching and should always be positive in order to motivate players. That is to say, give the impression that the performance was good in some way, but that it could be even better by changing and improving a particular part of the technique.   General rules are:

(i)   Be enthusiastic. If you are enthusiastic, this should be reflected in your voice. If you are enthusiastic in your manner, this will transfer to the players.

(ii)   Be clear and as simple as possible. Long-winded explanations, full of jargon and the presentation of more than one piece of information at a time, should be avoided.

(iii)   Only speak if you have something of value to say. Avoid 'commentating' on the action and in order to coach, stop the player from practising, so that you have his full attention.

(iv)   Think carefully about what you are going to say before you start speaking. This will ensure you give a clear, positive impression to the players.

(v)   Make sure you can be heard. This is less of a problem when speaking to an individual, than it is when speaking to a group which may be spread out. Take care to speak with the wind behind you whenever possible, rather than into it.

(vi)   Speak slowly and clearly. Don't forget that rushing your words will only make you more difficult to understand, especially for players further away.

(vii) Try to vary the pitch of your voice. If you speak with a boring, monotonous tone, this will give the impression that what you are saying is boring and monotonous.

(viii) Use eye contact when speaking. This not only holds the players' attention, but also gives you some feedback on whether you are being understood.

(B)   DEMONSTRATION.

It has been said that "a picture is worth a thousand words." Certainly, a picture in the form of a good demonstration will enable a player to see clearly the technique which he is being asked to do. Demonstrations have the advantage that they may consist of slow motion walk-throughs as well as those done at normal speed. General rules are:

(i)   The demonstration should be of good quality. Ideally, they should be done by the coach, although it is permissible to use one of the players. A good demonstration should inspire the players to achieve the same. Within reason a demonstration should be repeated until a good example is achieved.

(ii)   The demonstration should be clear and uncomplicated so that it will be fully understood. This may involve the whole technique or may highlight one particular part, for example, the stabbing action of the toe when chipping the ball.

(iii) The demonstration should be able to be seen easily by all the players. The best position for a demonstration will depend on what is being demonstrated, especially when a particular aspect of a technique is being shown in isolation. For example, the players may need to be behind the ball to see the position of the foot on contact. Avoid the players having to look into bright sunlight.

(iv)   The demonstration should be accompanied by short, simple instruction or explanation. This may direct the players' attention to a specific part of the demonstration.

Summary: Good communication tells and shows players what to do.

SMALL SIDED GAMES.

Once a particular technique has been practised in an individual or small group situation, it is vital that players are then given the opportunity to incorporate it into a game. Ideally, in order to give the maximum amount of practise and contact with the ball, such games should not be 11-a-side and instead, small sided games should be used. Indeed, there are strong arguments that all matches below the age of eleven should consist of small sided games.

Small sided games may be played with almost any number of players per side, provided that it is less than eleven, but between four and seven is most suitable and will bring the maximum benefit. Such games form the foundation upon which to develop players' techniques in realistic, competitive situations.

Many of the characteristics already outlined are relevant to coaching in small sided games, but because of the unique nature of such coaching, it has its own specific requirements which are outlined below.

1. ORGANISATION.

(i) Size of area.

Perhaps the most important aspect when organising small sided games is choosing the correct size of the area to be used. This will depend on 2 factors:

          (a) The number of players.
          (b) The age of the players.

(a) The number of players.

For a small sided game to be most effective it must reproduce as closely as possible, the elements of a full match. That is, the amount of time and space the players have should be realistic. For players over 16 years of age, the following sizes are recommended:

4 V 4	40 yards X 30 yards.
5 V 5	50 yards X 35 yards.
6 V 6	60 yards X 40 yards.
7 V 7	60 yards X 40 yards.

(b) The age of the players.

Where the players are below 16 years of age, the size of the areas given should be decreased. The following can be used as a rough guide:

6-11 years	4 V 4	30 yards X 20 yards.
	5 V 5	35 yards X 25 yards.
	6 V 6	40 yards X 30 yards.
	7 V 7	45 yards X 35 yards.
12-16 years	4 V 4	35 yards X 25 yards.
	5 V 5	40 yards X 30 yards.
	6 V 6	50 yards X 35 yards.
	7 V 7	50 yards X 35 yards.

The areas can be marked out using coaching cones or flag poles and as far as possible, the normal rules of the game should apply. Once players are aware of the intricacies of the offside rule, this also should be applied to avoid players developing the bad habit of lurking in offside positions.

(ii) Size of goals.

Goals should as far as possible be full size, although for the youngest players this might mean being 5 yards wide. This size should be increased to 6, 7 and finally 8 yards (for players 12 years and over). Large goals should be used primarily so that more goals are scored and therefore excitement is increased. They will also encourage players to take their shooting opportunities, rather than decline them due to the low chances of success when skittles or small goals are used. From the goalkeeper's point of view, large goals will heighten the need for them to develop the technique of good positioning and narrowing the angle at an early age.

(iii) Use of goalkeepers.

For the reasons stated in (ii) above, goalkeepers should always be used. If necessary, outfield players can take turns acting as the goalkeeper.

(iv) Use of bibs.

Coaching bibs or different coloured shirts should be used, so that both coach and players can easily distinguish one team from another during small sided games. If these are not available, it is possible to make things easier by putting all the players with dark shirts on the same team.

2. OBSERVATION.

(i) The coach should adopt a position from which to see the group and the individuals within it. As already stated, this is best achieved from the edge of the group and in the case of small sided games this must therefore be done from the touchline. Such games can be officiated satisfactorily from there and it prevents the coach getting in the players' way. The advantages of being able to see the whole playing area and players cannot be overstated.

(ii) When coaching in the game, even with only 4 players a side, there is a great deal of movement which makes this type of coaching much more demanding than coaching techniques to individuals. In order to simplify this complex picture, it is essential that only one of the teams is chosen for coaching purposes. This will immediately half the number of players on which the coach must concentrate his attention.   The other team should, of course, be encouraged to listen to and learn from what is being coached. This is particularly important where all the players are from the same club and normally play together as a team. The make-up of the 'coached' team should be decided by the coach, so that particular players in need of specific coaching can be targeted.

(iii) Even when only coaching one team of 4 players, the amount of movement in a game situation will be great. It is therefore recommended that in the early stages of coaching, only one aspect of a coaching topic is selected. An example of this might be to focus on putting pressure on the player with the ball, within a coaching session on defending. Defending has many components and in trying to deal with such a wide subject, there is the danger that players will become confused and that little progress will be achieved.

3. COMMUNICATION.
A) VERBAL INSTRUCTION.

(i) During the excitement and noise of a game, whether small sided or not, many players rarely hear anything except players around them shouting. In such circumstances, it is very unlikely that players will hear, let alone take any notice of, instructions from a coach. It is vital therefore, that when coaching is to take place, for it to be effective, play must first be stopped.

In order to stop a game, a clear, concise signal must be given. The normal signal for play to stop is a whistle, as used by referees. A loud blast on a whistle may also be used by a coach, provided the game is not being controlled with a whistle, as this could cause confusion. The alternative to a whistle is for the coach to use his voice, which will need to be loud and powerful. A shout of 'stop' is all that is required, repeated if necessary.

(ii) Whichever method of stopping the game is chosen, the intention is that the players' positions should be frozen, similar to the 'freeze-frame' facility on a video recorder. This will enable the exact situation which was recognised by the coach to be retained so that appropriate coaching can take place. This is important because players must develop the ability to recognise certain situations and react to them accordingly. At this level, when to use a technique may well be more relevant than the coaching of the technique itself.

(iii) Once the game is stopped, coaching may take place either from the touch-line or from the field of play. As with coaching in grid situations, coaching in small sided games must be directed at two levels - the individual and the group. However, because coaching in the game frequently relates to aspects of decision-making and teamwork, as well as technique, it is normal that even when an individual is being coached, the group should be able to hear the coaching points being made. That should help ensure that repetitive explanations are unnecessary and clarify to all the players what is required of them during the session. In such situations, the manner of the coach should be positive, pleasant and persuasive, as it is essential not to alienate players who may have been the subject of criticism during the session. As with coaching in grids, praise and enthusiasm should be used whenever appropriate.

(iv) As with all coaching, instructions should be kept brief and as simple as possible to avoid confusion.

B) DEMONSTRATIONS.

When coaching in the game, demonstrations may be of technique, but are more often related to decision-making, either technique selection or more likely an aspect of positional play. Once the game is stopped, the coach has the opportunity to do walk-through demonstrations or adjust the positions of players whilst making coaching points.

2. PASSING.

Mark Wright (England) uses good 'vision' and looks up to assess his passing possibilities.

Soccer is a game based on passing. It has been said that unless you can pass the ball well, it is unlikely that you will play at a high level. It follows therefore that it is important to practise a wide range of passing techniques in order to cope with any situation that might occur during a game.

As with techniques in most sports, in soccer some are more difficult to master than others. Logically, players will display different levels of mastery in techniques, depending on their previous experience and on their particular aptitude for that technique. When coaching, it is vital that these factors are taken into account and that practices are planned and adjusted if necessary to suit the ages and ability of the players. Practice will not make perfect, but it will make permanent. It is therefore essential that practice is frequent and correct. Indeed, once a high level of perform-ance has been reached, practice will have little effect, other than to maintain a player's current level, but where a player's level of performance is not high, frequent and correct practice will ensure they improve. However, being good technically does not itself make you a good player, there are still other considerations:

PASSING QUALITIES AND DECISIONS.

1) CHOICE OF PASS/PASS SELECTION.
Given that good technique will produce an accurate pass, the other main consid-eration is the choice of pass. Selecting the correct technique and performing it well in a match situation makes a technique into a skill and is the mark of a skilful player. The choice of pass must meet the needs of the situation. A player has 2 main choices:
(a) Air v Ground, (b) Feet v Space.

(a) Air v ground.
Lofted passes travel in an arc and therefore take longer than ground passes struck with the same pace. This allows opponents more time to react. Ground passes should be used whenever possible as they are quicker and easier to control, but lofted passes will be necessary when defenders are between the passer and target, or when the pass is likely to be intercepted if it is made on the ground.

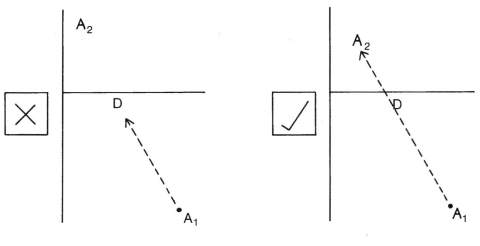

Ground pass intercepted.   Lofted pass successful.

(b) Feet v space.

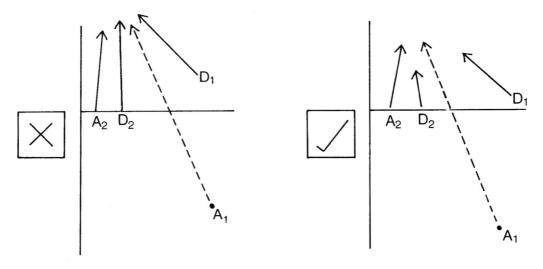

Pass played late and is intercepted.   Early pass is successful.

In tight situations the ball is almost always played to feet as this will help retain possession. If the momentum of an attack is to be maintained, however, the ball will often have to be played into space for a teammate to run onto. The problem is that defenders will try to 'read' such passes and be first into the space where the ball has been played. Provided the receiving player is ready, the sooner a ball is played, the less time opponents will have to react.

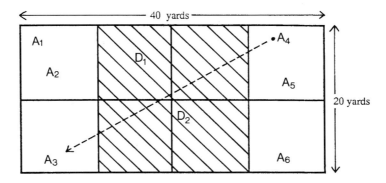

The A's interpass before making a pass through or over the D's to team-mates at the opposite end. All passes within the ends should be on the ground for speed and to make control easy. Whenever possible, passes to the opposite end should be on the ground to make control easier. If defender 'D' is in the direct line of pass, then it must be lofted over. The D's are restricted to the shaded area.

(2) TIMING OF A PASS.

A pass should be made when it will give maximum advantage to your team. If it is made too soon, the receiver may not have the chance to get into position or may be under pressure when receiving it. If it is made too late, it may be blocked or intercepted, or team-mates may run offside.

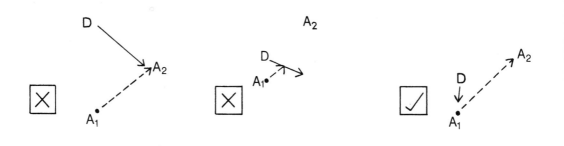

Pass made too soon.   Pass made too late.   Correct timing.

(3) DISGUISE.

Although it is not always vital to disguise your passes, whenever you do, it is likely that your pass will have more chance of reaching its target and also that the receiver will have more time and space. This is because opponents will themselves will have less time to react and can only do so once the ball has been played. This provides a big advantage which should not be overlooked. Most top players have the ability to disguise their intentions.

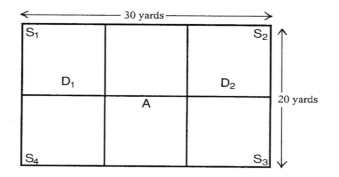

The ball is played from any of the servers (S) to 'A', who controls and tries to pass or dribble to any of the S's. The D's try to intercept. Key factors:

1. The importance of the first touch.
2. 'A' must disguise his intentions so that the D's cannot intercept:
     (a) Looking at one player and passing to another.
     (b) Pretending to pass, then dribbling.
     (c) Pretending to dribble, then passing.

(4) VISION.

No matter what passing skills a player has, without the vision to assess his passing possibilities he will be unable to make full use of them. All passing decisions should be based on the constantly changing positions of opponents and team-mates. Good players develop the ability to play with their heads up, so that at any time they know the positions of opponents and team-mates, sometimes even before they receive the ball. This will ensure that they are fully aware of all the available options.

The A's try to keep possession from D's, 6 v 2 in four grid squares. The receiving player should have time and space to control and observe the position of opponents and team-mates before selecting and delivering a pass. This can be extended to half a pitch with larger numbers, but still favouring one team, for example 9 v 3, or 8 v 4. As the players develop confidence and awareness on the ball, the situation can be made more even, e.g. 7 v 5 or 6 v 6, although this will probably be after many practice sessions.

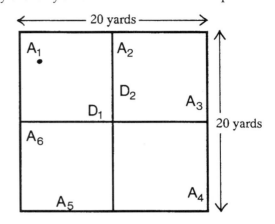

(5) WEIGHTING/PACE.

All of a player's previous good work may be undone by a badly weighted pass. The ball should be played as gently as possible, whilst still guaranteeing that it will reach its target and produce the maximum advantage to your team. A ball played too hard may be difficult to control and if played into space is likely to run out of play or to an opponent. A ball played too softly will often be intercepted and will give opponents time to react and recover. A major reason for attacks breaking down in and around the penalty area is passes being played too hard and either running out of play or to the goalkeeper.

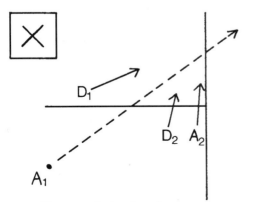

Pass made too hard.

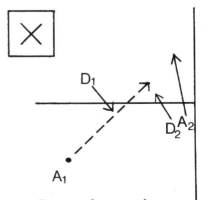

Pass made too soft.

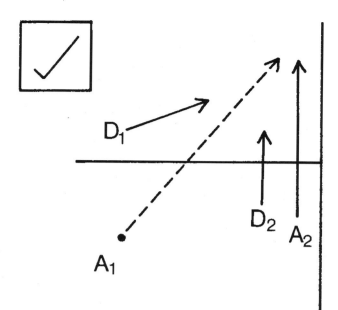

A pass correctly weighted, beats the defenders, but does not run out of play.

A good practice for the weighting of passes is shown in the diagram. A2 runs towards the open corner of the grid. A1 passes so that the ball arrives at the corner when A2 does. A2 then passes to A1, as A1 runs to an open corner of the grid. The ball should not leave the square and the receiving player should not have to wait for the ball to arrive.

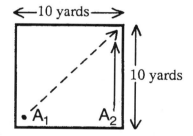

PASSING TECHNIQUES.

Within many of the following practices players will have the opportunity of improving their passing ability, not only in relation to technique, but also in respect of the other considerations mentioned above. Irrespective of the chosen technique, practice situations should be set up which will help improve the other qualities essential to skilful passing.

1. THE PUSH PASS.

The majority of passes made in a game are short passes along the ground. The most reliable passing technique for this is the push pass, which uses a pendulum action and is often the first technique which a young player learns. The principal objective of a push pass is to retain possession and only rarely will it create a major threat to a defence, therefore it is not recommended that possession football should be chosen as a team's main attacking strategy.

BENEFITS.

1. It is a reliable pass as there is a large area of contact which helps accuracy.

DRAWBACKS.

1. Easy for opponents to read.
2. Only useful for short distances.
3. Difficult to make on the move.

WHAT TO PRACTISE.

1. Non-kicking foot close to the side of the ball, pointing towards target.
2. Kicking foot turned outwards.
3. Inside part of foot contacts midline of ball.
4. Ankle firm.
5. Head down and steady, eyes on ball.
6. Follow through.

Before contact.

After contact

HOW TO PRACTISE.

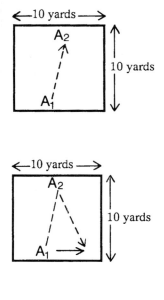

1. Work in pairs and pass the ball to each other. Use one touch to control the ball just in front of you and one to pass. Try to make your pass before the ball has stopped moving.

2. After passing move along your grid line. After controlling the ball, check the position of your partner before passing back to him. Condition the players:
   - (i) Control & pass with same foot.
   - (ii) Control & pass with different feet.
   - (iii) Control & pass with same part of foot.
   - (iv) Control & pass with different parts of foot.

   If you make 20 passes without the ball going out of the square, try first time passing, without controlling the ball. If the pass is wayward or too hard, control first before passing back and resuming one-touch.

3. Develop to 4 v 1, passing to team-mates while keeping the ball away from an opponent 'D'. If the players are very young or have poor technique, a bigger area (15 yard square), or larger odds (6 v 1) may be needed. Try to make 10 passes without the opponent touching the ball or it going out of the square.

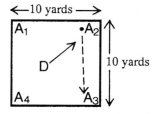

   Use no more than two touches each time and the player who receives the 10th pass goes in the middle. Passes should be made round the edge of the square, rather than across the middle where the opponent is.

   The timing of the pass is now important. Try to draw the opponent to you before passing, but not so close that the pass is blocked. Correct weighting and disguise will also greatly help the receiver. One of the players may be conditioned to use only one touch.

4. With 3 versus 1, the same points apply but the player who does not receive the pass must quickly move to the open corner, so that the receiver still has two passing chances along the lines of the grid.

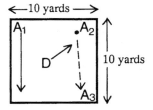

5. In this practice the D's cannot leave the grid, nor the A's enter it. A's can move along their grid lines, all passes must cross at least part of the grid. The player in possession normally passes to the free team-mate and the pass is determined by the movement of the defenders. If the defenders cover A2's nearest options, the ball can be played between them to A4. This type of penetrative pass should be encouraged. Interpassing between players near to each other, e.g. A1 and A2, will cause the defenders to react and may itself create the chance to pass it between them.

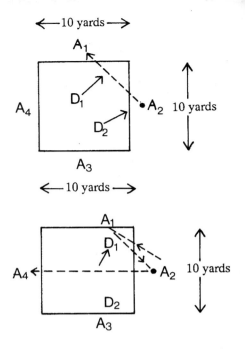

6. Again 4 v 2, but now all the players are inside a 15 yard square.

7. In a slightly larger area 3 versus 2 will produce a challenging situation for most players. Much of the success of this practice will depend on players off the ball getting into good positions to receive it. One possible move for A3 is marked on the diagram. The difficulty can be increased by conditioning one of the A's to play the ball on the first touch.

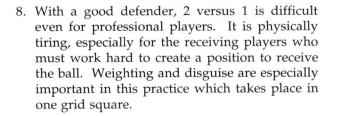

8. With a good defender, 2 versus 1 is difficult even for professional players. It is physically tiring, especially for the receiving players who must work hard to create a position to receive the ball. Weighting and disguise are especially important in this practice which takes place in one grid square.

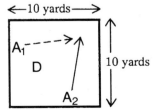

2. THE LOW DRIVE.

Once the push pass has been reasonably mastered, it becomes necessary to learn other passing techniques. One such technique for passing on the ground is the low drive, which is often used when shooting.

BENEFITS.

1. It is easy to disguise.
2. It is difficult for opponents to read.
3. It can be used over short and long distances.
4. It can be made on the move.

DRAWBACKS.

1. The small area of contact makes accuracy difficult.

WHAT TO PRACTISE.

1. Fairly straight approach to the ball.
2. Non-kicking foot close to the ball.
3. Head down and steady, eyes on the ball.
4. Ankle of kicking foot firm, with toes pointing down on contact.
5. Strike the centre of the ball with the laces part of the foot (instep).
6. Follow through. (This should depend on the power initiated.)

Before contact.   After contact.

HOW TO PRACTISE.

As with all techniques, the point of contact on the ball will decide whether it stays on the ground or rises in the air. To stay on the ground, contact must be through or above the midline of the ball. The initial emphasis must be placed on technique rather than on power, as the temptation to try this before mastering the basics will be great. Once the player's technique is good over short distances, the opportunity should then be given for practice over long distances.

Practices similar to those for the push pass can be used for the low drive. The organisation for these practices is the same as for practices 1 and 2 for the push pass except the area is increased to 30 yards by 10 yards and cones may be used to make a 3 yard target through which the ball should be played. (Passing the ball first time may not be possible owing to the pace of the ball).

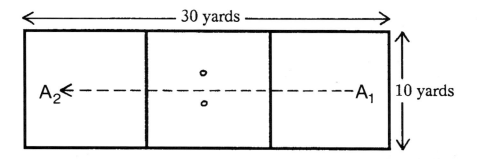

As the players' technique improves, the cones may be narrowed to 2 yards apart. As the low drive is one of the main techniques used when shooting, a full size goal and goalkeeper can now be introduced and the organisation is exactly the same as used for shooting (see p62).

3. THE LOFTED DRIVE.

For reasons already stated, whenever possible passes will be made on the ground. However, many times in a game this is not possible, as opponents are in the way and for a pass to be delivered successfully, the ball must be played in the air. Players must therefore practise the technique of passing the ball in the air. One of the most common techniques for passing long distances in the air is the lofted drive. It should be noted that for all lofted passes the point of contact on the ball must be below the midline in order to make the ball rise.

There are four main types of lofted drive. There are two techniques which use the laces (instep) - one with a wide approach, the other with a straighter approach to the ball. The other two, more difficult techniques, use the inside and outside of the foot in order to swerve the ball.

A. LOFTED DRIVE FROM A WIDE APPROACH USING THE INSTEP.
BENEFITS.
1. Can be used over long distances.
2. The ball can be made to rise quickly.
3. Backspin can hold the ball up for a team-mate on landing.
DRAWBACKS.
1. The ball has a high flight path and so allows opponents time to react.

WHAT TO PRACTISE.
1. Approach the ball from about 45 degrees.
2. Non-kicking foot should be 12 to 18 inches to the side of the ball and behind it.
3. Head down steady, eyes on the ball.
4. Ankle of kicking foot firm, with toes pointing down on contact.
5. Strike the centre of the ball, below the midline with the laces part of the foot (instep).
6. Follow through.

Before contact.

After contact.

B. THE LOFTED DRIVE WITH A STRAIGHT APPROACH USING THE INSTEP.

BENEFITS.

1. Can be used over long distances.
2. The ball has a low flight path, so doesn't allow opponents much time to react.

DRAWBACKS.

1. The ball rises slowly so may be easily blocked.
2. It is difficult to execute.
3. The ball has no backspin and so runs away on landing.

WHAT TO PRACTISE.

1. Approach the ball from 20 to 25 degrees.
2. The non-kicking foot should be 3 to 12 inches to the side of the ball and behind it.
3. Head down steady, eyes on the ball.
4. Ankle of the kicking foot should be firm, with toes pointing down on contact.
5. Strike the centre of the ball below the midline with the laces part of the foot (instep).
6. Follow through.

Before contact.   After contact.

C. THE LOFTED DRIVE WITH THE INSIDE OF THE FOOT.

Driving the ball is a difficult technique made more so when the inside of the foot is used and the ball is struck off-centre to make it swerve. Few players can perform this technique effectively.

BENEFITS.
1. It can be used over long distances.
2. It is difficult to read.
3. The ball can be made to rise quickly.
4. The ball can be swerved away from opponents.
5. The ball can be swerved into the path of team-mates.

DRAWBACKS.
1. The ball may have a high flight path and allow opponents time to react.
2. The ball has no backspin and so runs away on landing.

WHAT TO PRACTISE.
1. A slightly angled approach to the ball.
2. The non-kicking foot is to the side of the ball and behind it.
3. Head down and steady, eyes on the ball.
4. The ankle of the kicking foot is firm, toes pointing down on contact.
5. Strike off-centre of the ball, below the midline with the front part of the inside of the foot (where the big toe joins the foot).
6. The foot sweeps away from the body and through the ball from inside to outside in a rotating motion.

Before contact

After contact.
(The ball starts out to the right, but will
swerve back on target.)

D. THE LOFTED DRIVE WITH THE OUTSIDE OF THE FOOT.

Driving the ball in the air using the outside of the foot and striking the ball off-centre to make it swerve, is arguably one of the most difficult techniques in the game. The benefits and drawbacks are similar to those for striking with the inside of the foot.

BENEFITS.
1. It can be used over long distances.
2. It is difficult to read.
3. The ball can be swerved away from opponents.
4. The ball can be swerved into the path of team-mates.
5. The ball will have a low flight path, so it doesn't allow opponents time to react.

DRAWBACKS.
1. The ball rises slowly, so may be easily blocked.
2. The ball has no backspin and so runs away after landing.
3. It is very difficult to execute.

WHAT TO PRACTISE.
1. A fairly straight approach to the ball.
2. Non-kicking foot to the side of the ball and behind it.
3. Head down steady, eyes on the ball.
4. Ankle of the kicking foot firm, toes pointing down on contact.
5. Strike the ball off-centre, below the midline with the front part of the outside of the foot.
6. Foot sweeps across the body and through the ball from outside to inside.

Before contact.   After contact.

29

HOW TO PRACTISE.

The organisation of the technique practices for all four types of lofted drive are identical. The distances shown may be reduced for young players or those initially with poor technique. Similarly, they may be increased for players of exceptional ability. There should be the opportunity to practice with either foot and players should rotate positions frequently.

1. A1 and A2 work in the end grid. S1 works in the two centre grids. S1 passes the ball on the ground to A1, who makes a lofted pass to A2. The ball should land in A2's square. The pass from S1 should be gentle to allow A1 and A2 to establish the technique. (For the wide approach technique S1 should pass the ball towards the end corner of the grid, so A1 and A2 approach the ball at the correct angle.) Once A2 receives the ball, he passes to S1, who has followed the flight of the ball. S1 returns the pass and the practice is repeated.

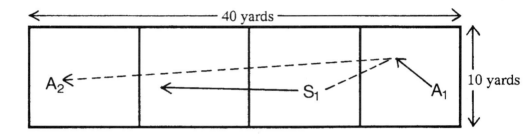

2. Once the players' technique is sufficiently good, S1 should put pressure on by trying to intercept the lofted passes, but staying in the middle two grids. Allowing S1 to use his hands will provide some protection from powerfully driven passes.
3. The practice may progress to being continuous, with all players being asked to use only one touch whenever possible.
4. An additional player S2 is introduced. S1 and S2 are restricted to the two centre grids and must try to intercept the lofted passes as S1 did before. S1 starts the practice by passing to A1, who controls the ball and makes a lofted pass to A2. A1 and A2 then inter-pass, each time using two touches - one to control and one to pass. As the ball is now being struck when it is moving away from the players, it will be more difficult to get the ball in the air.

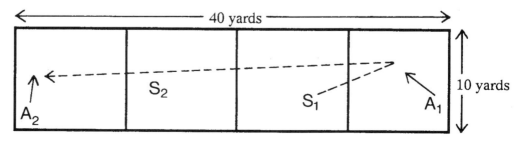

4. SWERVING THE BALL.

In addition to swerving the ball when making lofted passes, it is also possible to swerve the ball whilst keeping it fairly low, although the ball may still travel some of its distance in the air. This technique uses the inside or outside of the foot to swerve the ball and is particularly valuable when shooting. The only difference between this technique for swerving and those already discussed under lofted passes, is in the foot's point of contact on the ball. In order to keep the ball low it must be struck through the midline, but slightly to one side in order to make it spin. The points of contact for a right-footed player are shown in the diagrams below. All of the other coaching points for swerving the ball are the same as those given under lofted passes for the inside and outside of the foot.

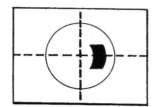   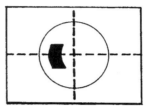

Inside of the foot.   Outside of the foot.

INSIDE OF THE FOOT.
BENEFITS.
1. Can be used over short and long distances.
2. The ball can be swerved away from or round opponents.
3. It is difficult to read.
4. The ball can be swerved a great deal.
5. The ball is spinning and difficult for a goalkeeper to hold.
6. The ball can be swerved into the path of team-mates.
DRAWBACKS.
1. When used as a pass, its flight may be harder to judge and it may be difficult to control.

OUTSIDE OF THE FOOT.
BENEFITS.
1. It can be used over short and long distances.
2. It is difficult to read.
3. The ball can be swerved away from or round opponents.
4. The ball can be swerved into the path of team-mates.
5. The ball is spinning and difficult for a goalkeeper to hold.
DRAWBACKS.
1. When used as a pass it may be difficult to control.
2. It is difficult to execute.

HOW TO PRACTISE.

1. A1 and A3 pass to A2 and A4, swerving the ball with the chosen part of the foot, inside or outside. The amount of swerve can be judged more easily by passing down the grid lines. Players are likely to find the inside of the foot technique easier to learn.

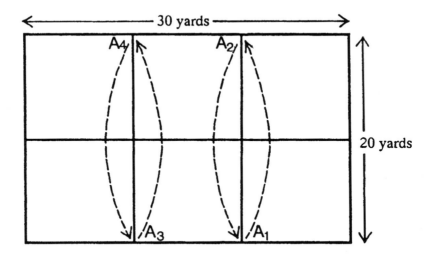

2. Once some degree of competence has been achieved, an opponent (passive at first), may be introduced to threaten the pass by standing on the intersection of the grid lines between passer and receiver.

3. The technique of swerving the ball may also be used in the practices for the push pass and shooting, in order to encourage its use as soon as possible.

5. THE FLICK PASS.

In tight situations, with your back to goal and when closely marked by an opponent, the flick pass can be a very effective attacking weapon. It can be used to pass the ball through almost 180 degrees, thus changing the angle of attack. It can also be heavily disguised and therefore opponents are unable to react until after the ball has been played.

BENEFITS.
1. It can be easily disguised.
2. It can be performed with a minimum of movement.

DRAWBACKS.
1. The pass is made blind, so the outcome is difficult to assess.
2. It is only useful for short distances.

WHAT TO PRACTISE.
1. Non-kicking foot to the side of the ball and behind it.
2. Ankle of kicking foot firm but flexible, toes pointing down.
3. Strike the midline of the ball at the side with the outside part of the foot.
4. The foot rotates outwards on contact, flicking the ball.
5. Move off in the opposite direction to the pass and look for a possible return.

Before contact.

After contact.

HOW TO PRACTISE.

1. S1 passes on the ground to A1 who plays a flick pass to either A2 or A3 who may move along their grid lines. They play the ball to S2 and the practice is repeated. Rotate the positions of the players frequently.

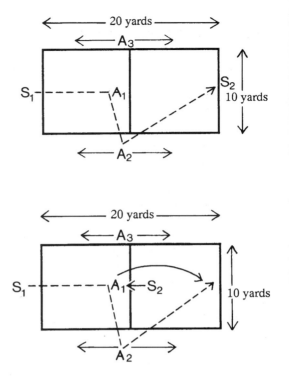

2. As soon as the players are performing the technique correctly, S1 and S2 alternate as opponents when the ball is played from the opposite end. A1 plays a flick pass to A2 or A3 and spins away from his marker to receive the return pass. If the opponents do not mark tightly, A1 should turn with the ball, having been given information by the server.

3. Practice 2 is repeated, with the area extended to 30 yards and a goalkeeper introduced.The practice should finish with a shot from A1, who should create the chance either by a flick pass or by turning with the ball.

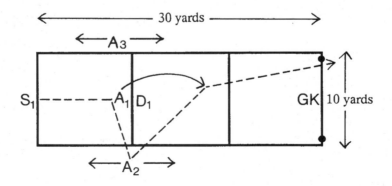

6. CHIPPING THE BALL.

As an attack moves further into the opponents' half of the field, the amount of space behind the defence is gradually reduced. If lofted passes as previously discussed are used to play the ball over the defence, it is likely that the ball will run out of play or be intercepted by the goalkeeper. In this instance, chipping the ball is an ideal technique.

BENEFITS.
1. The ball has a steep flight path, which enables it to clear even close opponents.
2. Backspin on the ball helps prevent it from running on to the goalkeeper or out of play.
3. It is difficult to read.

DRAWBACKS.
1. It can only be used over fairly short distances.
2. The ball will be spinning and may be difficult to control.
3. The high flight path allows opponents some time to react.
4. It is difficult to execute, even when the ball is rolling towards you.

WHAT TO PRACTISE.
1. A straight approach to the ball.
2. Non-kicking foot should be close to the side of the ball.
3. Head down and steady, eyes on the ball.
4. The kicking leg comes down steeply and sharply in a stabbing action.
5. The kicking foot should be firm, with toes drawn up on contact.
6. When the ball is opposite your non-kicking foot, strike the bottom of it with toes and laces.
7. There should be little follow through.

Before contact.
(Note steep backlift of kicking foot.)

After contact.
(Note steep path of ball.)

35

HOW TO PRACTISE.

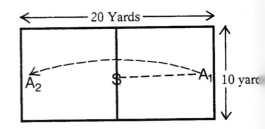

1. S1 passes the ball so it rolls gently, straight to A1, who chips the ball over S1 to A2. A2 then takes a return pass from S1 and repeats the practice by chipping to A1. The ball should have enough height to clear S1 and enough backspin to keep it in the grid and need the minimum of control from A1 and A2.

2. Once the players are showing satisfactory technique, the practice should be repeated with A1 and A2 controlling the ball with the first touch and chipping it with the second. The players will find it much more difficult chipping a ball rolling away from them, but this may be required in a match situation.

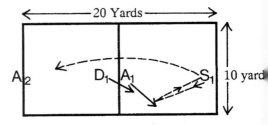

3. A1 moves towards S1, receives a pass and controls it. If D1 is not marking tightly, A1 turns and dribbles or passes to A2. If D1 is marking tightly, A1 plays the ball back to S1, who chips it over A1 and D1 for A1 to chase. The practice is then repeated from the other end, with A1 and D1 reversing their roles.

4. The practice is repeated, with the area extended to 30 yards and a goalkeeper introduced. Having collected the chip, A1 should finish with a shot. S1 may chip the ball on the first or second touch, depending on the quality of the return pass and on the positions of A1 and D1.

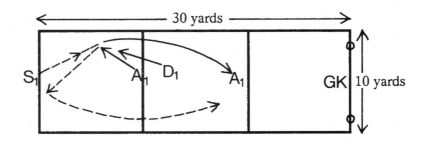

7. VOLLEYING.

When the ball is struck whilst in the air, the technique is known as volleying. Almost any part of the foot may be used, but the laces part (instep) is most common and gives the best control and power. In competitive situations, volleying is essential if the ball is to be played before an opponent can make a challenge. Volleying is a vital technique in and around both penalty areas for clearing the ball and for shooting.

The three main kinds of volley are the volley from the front, the volley from the side and the overhead or bicycle kick. For practice purposes, only the first two will be considered, as the latter is a development of the volley from the side, with the ball being taken at a higher point.

A. THE VOLLEY FROM THE FRONT.
BENEFITS.
1. The ball has a steep flight path which enables it to clear even close opponents.
2. The ball can be played powerfully over both long and short distances.
3. The ball often has topspin, which makes it dip.

DRAWBACKS.
1. It is difficult to get accuracy owing to the small point of contact.
2. When used as a pass, the topspin may make the ball difficult to control.
3. It is difficult to weight the pass correctly.

WHAT TO PRACTISE.
1. A straight approach to the ball.
2. The non-kicking foot should be behind the ball. The earlier the ball is played, the further away the non-kicking foot will be.
3. Head down steady, eyes on the ball.
4. The ankle of the kicking foot should be firm, toes pointing down.
5. Strike the ball centrally, below the midline, with the laces part of the foot (the instep). The exact point of contact will depend on how much height is needed.
6. Follow through.

On contact.

After contact.

HOW TO PRACTISE.

1. A1 serves himself and volleys the ball to A2 who returns it, also with a volley. At first, the ball may be dropped from the hands when volleyed, later it should be thrown up and allowed to bounce once and then volleyed. This gets the players used to adjusting their positions in relation to the ball.

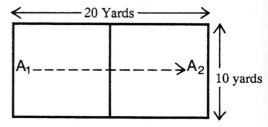

2. Once the players are competent over 20 yards, the practice area should be extended, first to 30 and then to 40 yards. The organisation is the same as above.

3. Two servers, S1 and S2 are then introduced in the middle two squares to throw the ball up for A1 and A2. Initially, the ball is volleyed after it has bounced once, but A1 and A2 are later encouraged to volley the ball before it bounces. A2 should control the ball and pass to S2 and the practice is then repeated. In both situations S1 and S2 put pressure on A1 and A2 by trying to intercept the volleys.

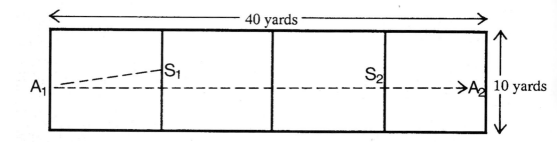

B.   THE VOLLEY FROM THE SIDE.
BENEFITS.
   1. The ball can be given a steep flight path which enables it to clear even close opponents.
   2. The ball can be played powerfully over both long and short distances.
   3. The ball can be taken high in its flight and contact made through the midline or above, so it is useful for shooting.
DRAWBACKS.
   1. It is difficult to get accuracy owing to the small point of contact.
   2. It is difficult to weight the pass correctly.
   3. Going for power rather than accuracy may cause the ball to rise too much.

WHAT TO PRACTISE.

1. Face the ball, sideways on to the intended line of flight.
2. Non-kicking foot should be well to the side of the ball.
3. Head down steady, eyes on the ball.
4. The ankle of the kicking foot should be firm, with toes pointed.
5. The kicking foot swings round in an arc as you pivot on the non-kicking foot.
6. Strike the ball at the side through the midline to keep the ball down for an attacking volley.
   Strike the ball at the side below the midline to make the ball rise for a defensive volley.   N.B. The point of contact determines the flight of the ball.
7. The higher you take the ball, the more you will fall away after volleying, leading ultimately to an overhead or bicycle kick.

Before contact.

On contact.

After contact.

HOW TO PRACTISE.

1. S1 serves to A1 who volleys to A2. S2 then serves to A2 and the practice is repeated. The organisation shown is for right foot volleys. For left foot volleys, the server should stand on the other side of the grid at S3 and S4. At first, the ball should be thrown up and allowed to bounce once and then volleyed. Later, A1 and A2 should attempt to volley the ball before it bounces. This practice is suitable for both attacking and defensive volleying.

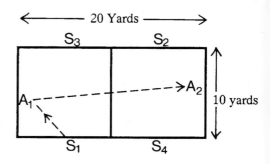

2. (Defensive volleying.) Once the players are competent over 20 yards the practice area should be extended to 30 and then to 40 yards. The organisation is as in 1 above. At no time should the ball bounce in the middle squares of these areas. Additional players D1 and D2 can be placed in the middle squares to put pressure on A1 and A2 by trying to intercept the volleys.

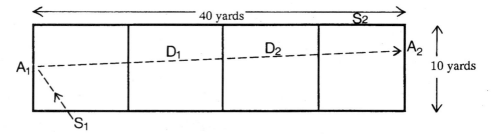

2. (Attacking volleying.) Once the players are competent the area should be extended to 30 yards and a goalkeeper introduced. The practice is continuous and works from end to end. A2 and S2 act as retrievers for A1. A1 and S1 act as retrievers for A2. Shots saved by the goalkeeper are passed to the opposite end of the grid.

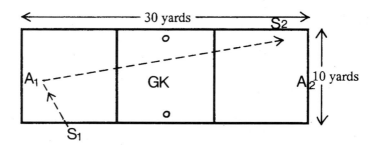

3. S1 and S2 may follow their service to put some pressure on A1 and A2 to take their shot as early as possible. Both players should follow in the shot in case of rebounds from the goalkeeper.

3. GAINING TIME ON THE BALL.

At any level of football, when players are given time they usually produce a better level of technique than when they are not given time. This is because in football, time means space. Defenders react to the movement of the ball, so it is normal that when a player receives the ball he is often already tightly marked or soon will be. Good players who receive the ball with time, often control it so they can pass or shoot before they are challenged. Good players, particularly when tightly marked, gain time for themselves to pass or shoot by :

      (1) Good control.
      (2) Feinting.
      (3) Dribbling.
      (4) Turning with the ball.
      (5) Running with the ball.

1. CONTROL.

Control is a means to an end. Good control on its own is of little value. Control must be used to enable a player to make a pass, dribble or shot. Almost any part of the body may be used, but the most common parts are foot, thigh and chest.

The two main types of control are :

      (a) cushion control and (b) firm or wedged control.

N.B. In both of these techniques, the success of the control will depend almost entirely on the quality of the first touch on the ball.

(a) CUSHION CONTROL.

As the name suggests, in cushion control all, or almost all the pace is taken out of the ball by the player, so that after control it remains very close. In a game players only rarely control the ball in this way, for example, when surrounded by opponents they need cushion control to keep the ball close and avoid losing possession.

(b) FIRM OR WEDGED CONTROL.

In firm control, only some of the pace is taken out of the ball by the player, or indeed sometimes pace may even be added to the ball. The result of this is that after control, the ball is moving away from the player. This is perfectly acceptable, provided it is moving in the required direction, at the correct pace and the player is moving quickly after it. This technique is used to best advantage when controlling the ball away from a particular opponent. This is done in order to increase or maintain the time the receiver has when he first gains possession.

WHAT TO PRACTISE.

Whether you wish to use cushion or firm control, it is the quality of the first touch which is all important. Six points are common to both:

1. Be alert and ready to receive the ball.
2. Be aware of the situation around you so, that you choose the correct means and direction for control - into space and away from your opponent.
3. Move into the line of the ball, and towards it if necessary, to control as soon as possible.
4. Keep the head steady and eyes on the ball.
5. Select the controlling surface (this will depend on the height of the ball).
6. Offer the surface to the ball.

CUSHION CONTROL

7. Keep the surface between opponent and the ball.
8. Withdraw and relax the surface on contact.
9. Resist the challenge from your opponent.

FIRM CONTROL

7. Angle the surface in the desired direction.
8. Slightly withdraw or thrust the surface on contact.
9. Move quickly after the ball.

Before controlling the ball on his chest, Mark Wright watches it carefully.
Note the arms helping his balance and the bent legs, ready to help absorb the pace of the ball, if necessary.

HOW TO PRACTISE.

1. CUSHION CONTROL.

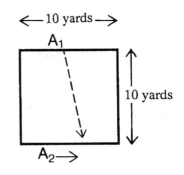

1. As cushion control is almost always used in tight situations, a practice area 10x10 yards is required. A1 and A2 start about 1 yard behind the end grid line. The ball should be served on the ground. On controlling, the ball should not go into the grid square. A1 passes on the ground wide of A2 who must move into line and control before passing back, wide of A1. Both players should control with the first touch, creating an angle to pass.

2. Once the players are competent on the ground, service should be made in the air so that the players have to select the controlling service. Because of the restricted area, the service may be thrown, or kicked from the hands.

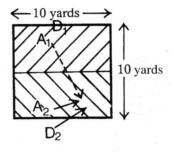

3. When the players are competent with ground and air control, opposition (D1 and D2) should be introduced. All the players are now inside the grid square. A1 serves the ball from his hands, on the ground or in the air, wide of A2. A2 must move and control the ball so that it remains inside his half of the grid, whilst preventing D2 from tackling for the ball. After controlling it, A2 may have to screen the ball, preventing D2 from reaching it by keeping his body in a sideways position, between D2 and the ball.
He should play the ball with the furthest foot from D2. A2 tries to keep possession for five seconds then makes a return pass to A1. The practice is then repeated with A1 keeping the ball from D1.

4. Free practice is allowed, but A1 and D1 and A2 and D2 must remain in their half of the grid. Whoever is in possession must keep the ball from their opponents by controlling and screening. A player is only allowed to keep possession for five seconds and the other player then must move into a position to receive the ball.

2. FIRM CONTROL.

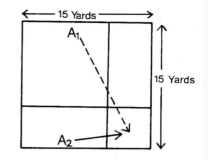

1. The practice initially takes place in an area 15x15 yards, but this may be increased if the standard of the players is high. A1 passes along the ground wide of A2, who must move into line and control before passing back wide of A1. Both players should control with the first touch, creating an angle to pass with the second.
   If the first touch is made fairly centrally, it should direct the ball forward and out towards the edge of the grid, but not out of the square. If the first touch is made close to the side of the square, it should prevent the ball going out of the square. The distance the ball is played on the first touch will depend on the situation and the speed of the player, but it is usually not more than two to three yards.

2. Once the players are competent on the ground, service should be made from the hands both on the ground and in the air so that the players have to select the controlling service.

3. Once the players are competent with ground and air control, opposition (D1 and D2) should be introduced and the area increased. Services should now be made off the ground. A1 passes to A2 and D1 and D2 judge whether control will be made in grid 1 or grid 2. As the pass is on its way, D1 moves to challenge if control is in grid 1. D2 moves to challenge if control is in grid 2. A2 controls the ball away from the challenging opponent and returns the pass to A1. The players return to their positions and the practice is repeated.

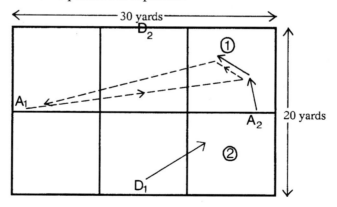

4. Once the players are competent, D1 or D2 challenge randomly as determined by a call from the server when he makes the pass. The receiver must now determine where the challenge is coming from, before controlling away from D1 or D2 and making a return pass.

A further practice may take place in a small area as follows:

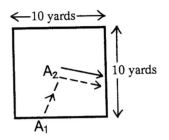

1. A1 serves on either side, wide of A2 who moves into line and controls the ball, taking it to the nearest side of the grid. The practice is repeated with A1 moving into the square and receiving the service from A2. Services should at first be on the ground and then in the air.

2. As soon as the receiver touches the ball, the server moves to challenge and prevent him from reaching the side of the grid. Speed is now important and the first touch must force the ball towards the line, so it can be stopped there with the second touch.

3. The server may now challenge as soon as he serves the ball. High slow services should be avoided, as the server then has an unfair advantage in preventing the receiver from reaching the line.

4. S1 and S2 serve a variety of balls to A1, who if possible should control with the first touch and shoot with the second. The service can land anywhere in the centre square and A1 has the choice of which goal to shoot at. He is not allowed to shoot from inside the centre square. The goalkeepers must stay on their line until A1 touches the ball and the length of the area may need to be increased for adults with good technique. If a retriever is positioned behind each goal, this will help the practice to run more efficiently.

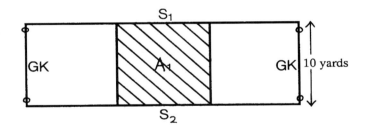

5. As soon as A1 touches the ball, the non-server moves to try and prevent him from taking a shot.

2. FEINTING.

Feinting means pretending to do one thing and then doing another. This can often gain you valuable time on the ball. If you are in possession, one example is pretending to pass or dribble and then not doing so. When feinting, the secret is to convince your opponent that your intention is genuine, because opponents react to what they think might happen. Players who use feints make their play unpredictable and thus make opponents uneasy whenever they get the ball.

WHAT TO PRACTISE.

(a) Feinting to Dribble.
1. Make a positive movement towards your opponent.
2. Pretend to play the ball past him in one direction.
3. Step over the ball and turn away in another direction with it.

(b) Feinting to Pass or Shoot.
1. Head down, concentrate on the ball.
2. Have a full back swing of the kicking leg.
3. Make sure your arm is thrown up as you move to strike the ball.
4. Swing the leg forward, stopping just before contact.
5. Turn away from your opponent with the ball.

HOW TO PRACTISE.

One versus one situations provide the best opportunity for players to practise feinting moves, but they can also be tried as an integral part of normal passing and dribbling practices and during small sided games. The key is for players to try moves on their own, slowly at first and to gradually build up speed as they gain in technique and confidence.

3. DRIBBLING.

Players who can dribble the ball well are a valuable attacking weapon. Generally, the closer you move to your opponent's goal, the less space there will be for the player in possession. A player who can beat an opponent in a tight situation in and around his opponent's penalty area may create a scoring chance for himself or his team. In that situation dribbling brings its greatest rewards. However, there is always the chance that dribbling may be unsuccessful and the dangers of losing the ball increase, the nearer you are to your own goal. This should be taken into account when deciding whether or not to dribble. Only a fairly low proportion of unsuccessful dribbles lead directly to lost possession, many others result in penalties, free kicks, corners or throws-in and so possession is maintained. The odds in favour of dribbling are perhaps higher than they first seem, although this will vary greatly, depending on an individual player's dribbling skill. An individual should try to develop competency in 2 or 3 moves, so that he can produce them at will during a game.

WHAT TO PRACTISE.
1. Keep the ball under close control using different parts of the foot.
2. Keep your head up to observe the positions of opponents and team-mates.
3. Use movement of the ball and your body to throw your opponent off balance.
4. Play the ball past your opponent, forcing him to turn.
5. Accelerate away.

John Barnes (Liverpool) accelerates away as he plays the ball past Martin Kuhl and Warren Neill (Portsmouth), during the 1992 F.A. Cup Semi-Final.

HOW TO PRACTISE.

1. Use a circle or square 10 yards across for up to 15 players, each with a ball. The players move around the area, concentrating on 1 and 2 above. They may be asked to concentrate on a particular foot or on a particular part of the foot and to respond to the coach's instructions, for example "stop" or "change" (direction). The players should try to keep the ball away from each other. With larger numbers of players or fewer balls, players can pair up and swap at regular intervals.

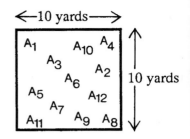

2. Once the players are familiar with control of the ball whilst keeping their head up, then some degree of opposition should be introduced. Initially this can be done in the above organisation by allowing the players to try and knock each other's ball out of the area or by allowing another player to act as a defender, with the last player in being the winner. The degree of opposition should be strictly controlled.

3. The players now work in pairs in the same sized area. 'A' tries to tag 'B', while they both keep control of their ball. Once tagged, they change roles. Emphasis now changes to key factor 3 above.

4. 'A' and 'B' face each other across a 10 yard line with cones at either end. 'A' starts in possession and tries to get to either cone before 'B'. 'A' should move the ball and his body to throw 'B' off balance and then play the ball towards the cone and accelerate after it. 'B' is not allowed to cross the line or tackle 'A', he can only put his foot on the cone before 'A' gets the ball there. The players should change roles frequently.

5. 'A' and 'B' now practice in a grid square. 'B' starts in the centre and passes to 'A' who is in a corner. 'A' meets the ball and attacks 'B', trying to get the ball to any of the other corners. 'B' is now free to tackle.

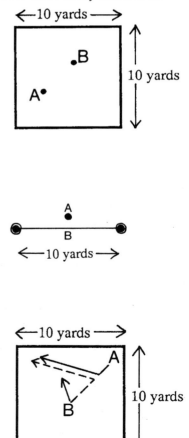

6. A full size goal and goalkeeper are now introduced. 'B' plays the ball to A1 who dribbles between the cones past 'B' and then tries to score. He may shoot past, or dribble around the goalkeeper, depending on the situation. Initially, 'B' defends the square in front of him. Later, he is allowed to move anywhere.

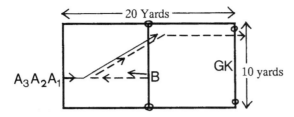

7. 4 v 4 in a 30 x 20 yard area. Players should be encouraged to dribble in order to create a shooting chance.

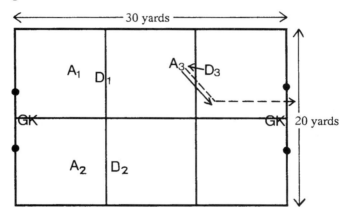

8. Dribbling can also be developed in small-sided or full games, which may be 'conditioned', for example, "whenever you get the ball in your opponent's half you must dribble." Care should be taken to ensure that such situations are not unrealistic.

4. TURNING WITH THE BALL.

If players receive the ball when not facing their opponent's goal, provided they are confident in their own skill, they should try to turn as quickly as possible, as this will provide the opportunity to shoot, pass or dribble the ball forward and offer the maximum threat to the opposition.

If a player is not tightly marked when he receives the ball, then turning is merely a matter of controlling the ball in the required direction with a good first touch. If a player is tightly marked, turning is a far more risky and demanding skill. Players who can turn with the ball in and around their opponent's penalty area are usually valuable members of their team. Some of the turning techniques shown here are best used when a player is moving across the field. Once he has made the turn and created space for himself, he can then complete the move by passing, running or dribbling the ball forward. An individual should try to develop competency in 2 or 3 moves, so that he can produce them at will during a game.

WHAT TO PRACTISE.

Whilst a wide range of turning techniques are possible, it is only necessary for a player to be competent at two or three. Almost all turns use either the inside, outside, or sole of the foot. Three examples of turning techniques are shown in the photographs.

1. A common feature of all turns is to keep a low centre of gravity. This will enable you to change direction quickly. The knees should therefore be bent.
2. Whenever possible, meet the ball to try and create space between you and your opponent.
3. Become familiar with using the inside, outside and sole of the foot in order to turn with the ball.
4. Try to disguise your intentions as much as possible.
5. Become familiar with the space around you when in possession, so that you don't turn away from one opponent and into another.
6. Accelerate quickly after the ball and away from your opponent, once you have made your turn.

The Inside Hook. The foot reaches outside the line of the body and the ball is hooked back with a firm touch, before pivoting and accelerating after it.

The Drag-Back. Reach outside the line of the body and drag the ball back by firmly rolling the sole of the foot across the top of the ball and pivoting on the other foot. Accelerate away after the ball (below).

The Cruyff Turn. (Named after the Dutch World Cup star who made it famous.) Pretend to kick the ball, throwing the arm up. Pull the ball back firmly behind the planted foot, using the inside front part of the foot. Accelerate away after the ball (below).

HOW TO PRACTISE.

(One type of turn should be attempted before moving onto another).

1. 'A' takes the ball to a line five yards away, turns and comes back. 'B' then takes over and repeats. The movement should first be done at walking pace to establish the pattern and the speed be increased gradually.

2. Once the basic technique has been mastered, 'A' and 'B' then work towards each other from opposite sides of the square. As they approach each other, they turn away from each other and return to their starting position. The turn should be made so that the player keeps his body between his opponent and the ball. Again, start slowly and gradually increase the speed.

3. 'A' plays the ball gently past 'B', who turns and chases it. 'A' runs after 'B' and goes round one side of him to try and get the ball. 'B' turns away from 'A' and back to the centre line. He then passes to 'C' and the practice is repeated.

4. 'A' starts with the ball and his back to 'B', who is not allowed to cross the line. 'A' tries to reach either of the sidelines before 'B' can get there. He can use any type of turn to throw 'B' off balance before accelerating away.

5. Progress to 2 versus 2 in an area 20 by 20 yards. S1 serves the ball to either of the B's who must turn and pass to S2. S2 then serves to either of the A's, who must turn and pass to S1.

6. As above, but S1 and S2 act as goal-keepers when they are not serving the ball.

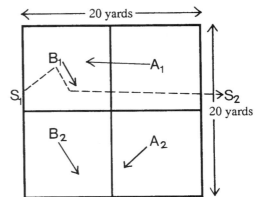
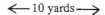

5. RUNNING WITH THE BALL.

Running with the ball is when the player in possession covers ground in which there are no opponents, the objective being to prevent defenders from getting into recovery positions goal side of the ball. The key element is therefore speed and the technique may only be used when there is space in front of you. It is frequently used when players are clear of the defence, going for goal. A player who is good at running with the ball will gain himself time by preventing pursuing players from catching him and getting goalside of the ball. A player should not run with the ball if he can pass to team-mates in more dangerous positions, or if the conditions are bad, for example, on a muddy or uneven surface.

WHAT TO PRACTISE.
1. Get the ball out from under your feet with a firm first touch.
2. Keep low, so you are quick off the mark.
3. Use the laces part of your foot, so you don't break your stride.
4. Have your head up, so you can observe the positions of team-mates and opponents.

Alan Shearer (England) runs with the ball, during the 1992 European Championship match against France. Note that the ball is out in front of him and his head is up to observe the positions of team-mates and opponents.

HOW TO PRACTISE.
N.B. These are strenuous practices and should be of limited duration.

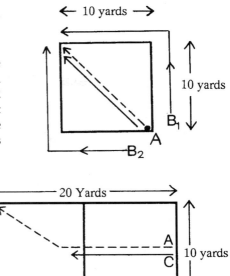

1. All three players start at the same corner. The ball is on the corner of the square. 'A' must run with the ball across the square, while B1 and B2 must go along the grid lines. B1 and B2 cannot move until 'A' touches the ball. Emphasise the key points given. The players rotate positions frequently.

2. 'A' runs with the ball to 'B', but is only allowed to touch the ball once in the first square. 'B' then runs with the ball to 'C' and the practice is repeated. Once the players have mastered the practice, the receiving player moves along his line to one corner. The running player must observe his movement and pass the ball to him.

3. Player 'A' sets off running with the ball, trying to touch the ball only once in each square. With the third touch, the ball should be passed between the cones, which are approximately two yards apart. Player 'E' plays the ball with a firm first touch and the practice is repeated.

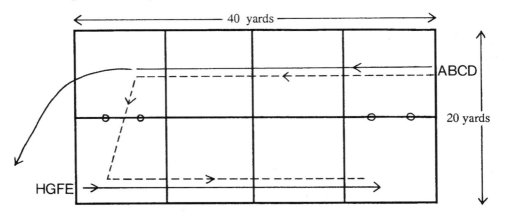

4. A pursuing defender is introduced, chasing from a cone placed 3 yards behind the end grid line. He may only move once the receiving player has touched the ball.

5. Small sided games may then be used to emphasise running with the ball. Whenever players receive the ball with space in front of them, they should be encouraged to move into that space as quickly as possible.

4. SHOOTING.

Gary Lineker (England) scores with a volley in a 1992 European Championship qualifying match against Poland.

It has been suggested that if a team can produce ten shots on target, they will never lose a match. If this is true, then it is a clear indication that shooting is of vital importance and therefore much time should be spent on improving this aspect of the game, particularly shooting on target, as often as possible . Before discussing shooting technique, there are three main considerations: 'when to shoot', 'when not to shoot' and 'where to shoot'.

A)   WHEN TO SHOOT.

Many opportunities for shooting arise in a game, but players may not recognise them, or decline the chance to shoot in favour of passing or dribbling. This is a mistake and there are only three instances when a player should even consider not shooting:

1)   When he is too far out.
2)   When a defender will block the shot.
3)   When the angle is too narrow.

If none of these conditions exist, then players should be encouraged to be alert and to take every shooting opportunity which presents itself. It should be regarded as a greater sin not to shoot, than to shoot and miss.

Players should **never** be afraid to shoot.

B) WHEN NOT TO SHOOT.

1. WHEN TOO FAR OUT.

At international level, some players are prepared to shoot from distances up to 40 yards. At lower levels, few goals are scored from that sort of distance. This could be because few shots are taken, or because of poor technique. What is clear is that beyond a certain distance, the chances of beating the goalkeeper are lower. This distance will depend on several factors, including the player's technique, the goal-keeper's technique and the weather conditions. With a strong wind behind him a player may have a better chance of scoring. It will be up to the player to assess his chances of success when deciding whether or not he is too far out.

2. WHEN A DEFENDER WILL BLOCK THE SHOT.

If a defender is so close that a shot is certain to be blocked, then a shot should not be taken. That does not mean that a shot should never be taken when a defender is between the player and the goal, merely that the distance away is important. Indeed, it is a positive advantage to shoot past defenders between the ball and the goal, as it is likely the goalkeeper will be unsighted and only be able to react late to the ball.

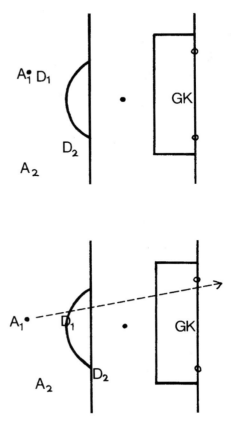

In this diagram, the defender D1 is so close to A1 that it is almost certain an immediate shot would be prevented or blocked. A pass or dribble would be a better alternative.

In this diagram, the defender D1 is between A1 and the goal, but not close enough to prevent or block the shot, which may be played round him. The goalkeeper is likely to be unsighted by his own defender, D1.

57

3. WHEN THE ANGLE IS TOO NARROW.

From narrow angles, the chance of scoring is reduced. In situations where the angle is narrow, if no team-mate is in a better position, the shot should still be taken in spite of a low chance of success. In situations where the angle is narrow and a team-mate is in a better position, the ball should be passed. Ideally, the pass should do two things:

    1) Eliminate the goalkeeper.

    2) Improve the shooting angle.

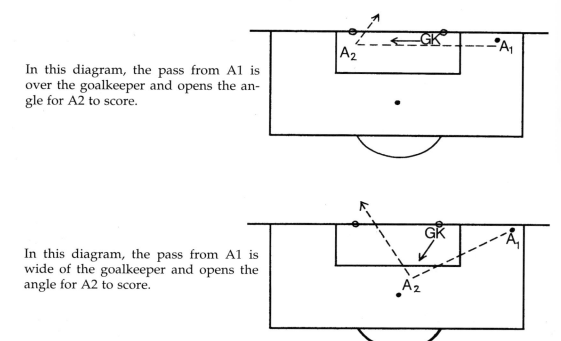

In this diagram, the pass from A1 is over the goalkeeper and opens the angle for A2 to score.

In this diagram, the pass from A1 is wide of the goalkeeper and opens the angle for A2 to score.

C) WHERE TO SHOOT.

When shooting, accuracy is the most important factor. It is vital that the shot is on target, forcing the goalkeeper to make a save. There are, however, certain parts of the goal which are more vulnerable than others when shooting. The first consideration must be the position of the goalkeeper.

1. WHEN THE GOALKEEPER IS BADLY POSITIONED.

If the goalkeeper is badly positioned, then clearly the shot should be made to that part of the goal where the goalkeeper will have the most trouble in making a save. When shooting, observing the position of the goalkeeper is very important and a player should do so whenever possible, before deciding where to shoot.

In this diagram, A1 passes to A2 who shoots into the open side of the goal before the goalkeeper can recover his position.

Here, A1 plays the ball over the goalkeeper to A2. While the ball is in the air, the goalkeeper moves across the goal to get into a good position to block the shot or header. A2 plays the ball back into the side of the goal the goalkeeper has come from, as it will be difficult for him to adjust his position and make a save.

2. WHEN THE GOALKEEPER IS WELL POSITIONED.

If the goalkeeper's position is good relative to the situation, then the shooter must still make it as difficult as possible for the goalkeeper to make a save. This can be done firstly, by shooting *low* and secondly, by shooting *to the far post.*

a) LOW SHOTS.

Many goalkeepers make spectacular saves from shots going into the top corner of the goal. In fact, these saves are relatively easy to make, compared with those going into the bottom corners. This is because the goalkeeper's hands and arms are already fairly close to the height of the ball and it is far easier to spring up quickly, than to get down quickly.

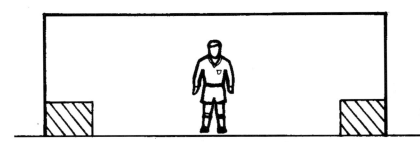

A low shot may also bounce or skid awkwardly, giving the goalkeeper a further problem when trying to save. It follows that shots to the bottom corners of the goal will normally provide the most problems for a goalkeeper and this should be a priority when shooting.

b) SHOTS TO THE FAR POST.

When shooting from any sort of angle, shots to the far post are likely to be more effective than shots to the near post for several reasons:

(i) Goalkeepers often make sure that they are not beaten at the near post and cover that area particularly well. This is probably because a near post goal is often regarded as a goalkeeper's error.

(ii) Shots made to the near post are easier to deflect out of play for a corner, because the distance to the goal line is short. This will give the defence time to organise and recover.

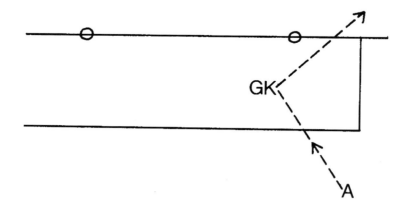

(iii) Shots to the far post are difficult to deflect out of play and therefore secondary scoring chances may fall to teammates in the area around the far post.

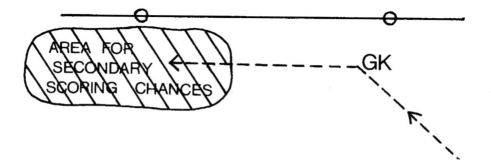

Players who are aware of these factors will greatly increase the chances of goals being scored, either directly, or as a result of another player's reaction to the shot.

SHOOTING TECHNIQUE.

WHAT TO PRACTISE.

A wide variety of shooting techniques may be needed, depending on the situation - the ball may be driven, volleyed, chipped or even push passed. All of these techniques are dealt with in the section on passing , as when you shoot, you should be trying to pass the ball into goal. Much of the skill in shooting comes from selecting the correct technique and then performing it well. It is vital that, at the moment of striking the ball, the player should be calm, composed and concentrate on making a good contact.

Once the decision to shoot has been taken and the correct technique applied, the priorities are:

1. ACCURACY.

Above all, when shooting, the major priority is accuracy. Provided a shot is on target, there is always a chance of scoring. The principle should be to force the goalkeeper into making a save and not allow him the luxury of letting a shot go for a goal kick.

Naturally, no matter how much players try, not every shot will end on target. If a shot is off target, it is better to be wide, rather than high. The reasoning behind this is that a shot going wide always has a chance of being deflected in, whereas one going over the bar has no such chance. As previously discussed, shots should in normal circumstances be kept low and aimed towards the far post, but of major importance when deciding where to shoot, is the position of the goalkeeper. Whenever possible, players should be encouraged to observe the position of the goalkeeper, before deciding where to shoot.

2. POWER.

Once players have gained accuracy in their shooting, the next priority is power. When a shot is on target and hit powerfully it will give the goalkeeper less time to react and therefore less chance of saving. A shot hit powerfully will also be more difficult to hold and if not going directly into goal, may lead to a secondary scoring chance for anyone following up.

3. SWERVE / SPIN.

Top level players will not only look to get accuracy and power in their shooting, but may also try to impart swerve or spin to the ball. This is for two reasons, firstly, in order to get the ball around opponents, including the goalkeeper and secondly, to make them increasingly difficult to hold. Whilst even the top players may find this difficult, most players who are technically sound will be capable of achieving some success if they practise. It is likely that such players will achieve most success when striking a dead ball, rather than a moving one and so they should perhaps limit their initial attempts to situations such as direct free kicks. Swerve and spin can, of course, be gained unintentionally, whenever the ball is mis-hit.

HOW TO PRACTISE.

In order to develop a positive attitude towards shooting, the practice situation should relate as closely as possible to that in a game, that is, there should be:

1. Full sized goals (small goals can discourage players from shooting for fear of missing).
2. A goalkeeper.
3. A moving ball (especially dropping and bouncing).
4. Opposition/pressure.
5. In all shooting practices there should be emphasis on being alert to the possibility of rebounds from either the post, crossbar, goalkeeper, or other players.

The suggested organisation for shooting practices is as shown below:

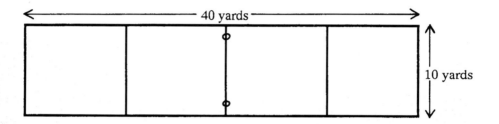

This organisation is ideal for practising a variety of shooting techniques. Because the goal is centrally placed and the goalkeeper faces different sides alternately, it does away with the need for retrievers. When more than one group is working at least a 10 yard space should be allowed between them to prevent wayward shots from hitting other players. Of course, shooting may also be effectively coached in the penalty area of a football pitch, but the above organisation is recommended for coaching large numbers of players in basic technique.

Apart from direct free kicks and penalty kicks, shots on goal are almost always taken from a moving ball and often from one which is dropping or bouncing. It is vital that shooting practices include this type of service, so that they relate as closely as possible to a game situation.

SHOOTING OPPORTUNITIES.

Shooting opportunities are of three main types:

        1. BALLS MOVING AWAY FROM YOU.
        2. BALLS MOVING ACROSS YOU.
        3. BALLS MOVING TOWARDS YOU.

Practice at all of these is necessary if players are to be expected to make the most of their shooting opportunities in a game. The above three types become progressively more difficult to perform successfully, therefore, in initial stages of learning, practice might be started with balls moving away from you, but players should be allowed to practise other types of shooting, even before they have mastered this first type. Similarly, a rolling ball will be easier to strike than one which is dropping or bouncing, therefore initially, practice may be with a rolling ball, but players should be allowed to practice with dropping or bouncing balls, even before they have mastered striking a rolling ball. As already stated, which shooting technique to select will depend on the situation, but is likely to be a drive or volley. (See Passing, pp24-40).

Gary Lineker (England) scores the equalizing goal in the 1990 World Cup Semi-Final against West Germany. The ball has moved across his body and Lineker has seized the opportunity to shoot, even though the ball is on his weaker left foot.

1. BALLS MOVING AWAY FROM YOU.

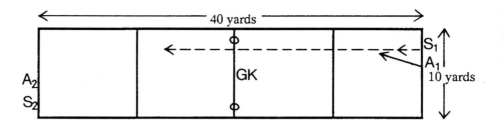

1. In the diagram , S1 plays the ball forward a few yards on the ground and A1 runs onto the ball and shoots. The practice is then repeated, with S2 serving to A2 from the other end. The low drive should be used. (See p.24.)

2. Once shooting technique is satisfactory, consideration should be given to the position of the goalkeeper. This should be done as the player runs onto the ball, observing where the goalkeeper is, just before shooting. This is important in helping the shooter decide not only where to shoot, but when to shoot.

3. Players should be shooting initially from 12-15 yards, so the situation is acceptable from the goalkeeper's point of view. This distance may be increased to 15-20 yards once a reasonable success is achieved from closer range.

4. Provided technique is satisfactory, dropping and bouncing balls should be served, so that volleying, as well as driving the ball is required.

5. In addition to varying the type of service, requiring the use of different techniques, pressure can also be introduced by the server chasing the shooter from behind. This is best done by placing a cone some 2-3 yards further back and starting the service from there. This equates to the situation in a game where the attacker is clear of the defence, but is being pursued.

6. Players should be given the opportunity to shoot with both feet by varying the side from which the ball is served.

2. BALLS MOVING ACROSS YOU.

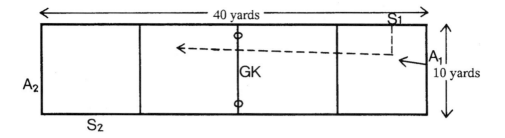

1. In the diagram, S1 rolls the ball gently across the grid and A1 runs onto it and shoots. The practice is then repeated, with S2 serving to A2. The low drive should be used. (See p.24.)

    The shooter should move quickly to the ball and not allow it to run across him. The shot should therefore be taken with the foot nearest to the side from which the ball has been served, i.e. right foot shot from the right, left foot shot from the left. Only if the player is unable to reach the line of the ball in time, should it run across him and the shot be taken with the other foot. This is because one of the major requirements in shooting is to be well-balanced and steady. This is much easier to achieve when shooting with the nearest foot, as the non-kicking foot can be planted and the body positioned much earlier. When allowing the ball to run across your body, the non-kicking foot is often placed too hurriedly and too far from the ball to ensure a high degree of accuracy. In spite of the mechanical weakness of this method, some players allow the ball to run across them, so that they are shooting with their preferred foot. This is a mistake not only mechanically, but also because it takes longer to execute and therefore has a greater chance of being blocked.

2. Shooting should initially be from 12 to 15 yards and then the distance increased.

3. Once the basic technique is satisfactory, shooters should be encouraged to check the position of the goalkeeper before striking the ball.

4. The type of service should be varied, with different shooting techniques being required and different feet being used.

5. Some pressure may be introduced to make the shooter move more quickly to the ball. This should be done by introducing additional players, who start at a cone two to three yards behind A1 and A2 and then chase them, once the ball is served.

6. As the ball is coming across you, for shots to the near side of the goal the body should be kept 'closed'. For shots to the far side of the goal, the body should be 'open'. On contact, the leading shoulder should point at whatever area of the goal has been chosen as a target.

3. BALLS MOVING TOWARDS YOU.

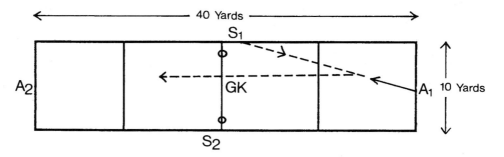

1. In the diagram, S1 rolls the ball gently towards A1, who runs on to it and shoots. The practice is repeated, with S2 serving to A2. The low drive should be used. Because the ball is rolling towards the shooter, it will be difficult to keep it down. Players should allow the ball to come as close as possible to their non-kicking foot and keep their head down until after contact, or the ball may rise over the bar.

2. Shooting should initially be from 12 to 15 yards and then the distance increased.

3. Once basic technique is satisfactory, players should observe the position of the goalkeeper just before shooting.

4. The type of service should be varied, requiring different shooting techniques.

5. Pressure may be introduced to make the shooter move quickly to the ball. This should come from additional players, who start at a cone two to three yards behind A1 and A2 and chase them, once the ball is served.

6. Players should be given the opportunity to shoot with both feet, by varying the side from which the ball is served.

7. If a goal with a net is available, the server may stand behind the goal and serve over the bar, for the attacker to run onto and shoot .

SECONDARY SCORING CHANCES.

In addition to the above practices for the three main types of shooting opportunity which arise in a game, time spent on heightening awareness of secondary scoring chances should bring high rewards, as a high proportion of goals are scored in this way. During any of the previous shooting practices, players should be alert to rebounds from the post and crossbar (if a proper goal is used), the goalkeeper, or other players. Within reason and with regard to players' safety, a practice should continue until the ball is 'dead' - behind the goal line, in the goalkeeper's possession, or out of the immediate area.

WHAT TO PRACTISE.

The number of secondary scoring opportunities created and taken can be increased if all players are made aware of the principles outlined in 2 above, in relation to shots made low and to the far post.

HOW TO PRACTISE.

1. In the diagram , the ball is served into a wide position in the penalty area for A1 to run onto and shoot first time. A2 starts at a cone on the opposite side of the penalty area and runs in towards the left hand post, as soon as the ball is served.

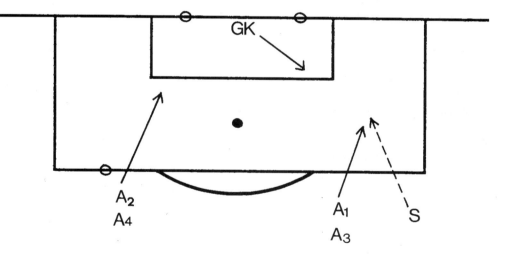

The shooter should observe the position of the goalkeeper before shooting and unless he has moved to anticipate a far post shot, that is the part of the goal for which to aim. A2 should be alert, not only to rebounds from the goalkeeper, but also to shots going across goal and wide of the post. A3 and A4 repeat the practice, allowing A1 and A2 to return to their starting positions. After five shots, change roles and then change to shooting from the left. Players should be made aware of the sin in shooting over the bar or wide of the near post. The starting position of A2 will need to be adjusted, dependent on the age and speed of the players.

2. Two recovering defenders may be introduced to put pressure on the attacking players.

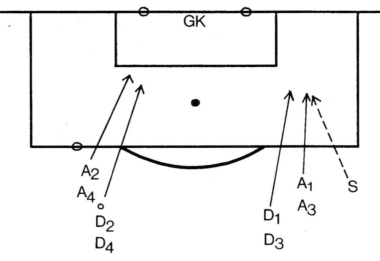

3. Finally, a further attacker and defender may be introduced to threaten and protect rebounds and shots in the central area of the goal.

4. Once the above principles are firmly understood, players can work on technique in small groups as shown in the diagram. The practice is 2 v 1 plus goalkeepers. The goalkeeper passes to A1 or A2 who dribble or interpass to get a shot. D1 defends against them and D2 is a retriever. Both A1 and A2 must follow up for rebounds, especially in the far post area and continue in possession as long as they score. When they fail to score D1 and D2 become attackers and A1 becomes a defender. Rotate the positions of the players.

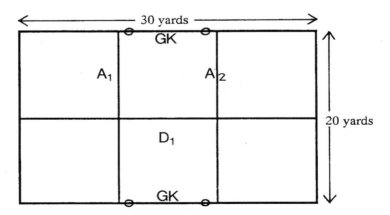

5. HEADING.

One of the most common ways of playing the ball past opponents is to play it over them. Heading is therefore an important aspect of Association Football, because players on both sides try and be first to the ball, particularly in the penalty areas, where defenders and attackers alike recognise the importance of playing the ball as early as possible and therefore of the value of good heading technique.

NB. Care should be taken that injuries due to clashes of heads are avoided in practice situations where heading is involved.

1. INTRODUCTION TO HEADING.

WHAT TO PRACTISE.

For heading the basic principles are:
1. Use the forehead.
2. Keep the eyes open.
3. Have firm neck and trunk muscles.
4. Contact the ball firmly, don't let it hit you.

HOW TO PRACTISE.

1. In pairs, one ball between two, standing two to three yards apart. Hold the ball in front of your face with bent arms. With one foot in front of the other, lean back then bring your weight forward onto the front foot, heading the ball out of your hands to your partner. The practice is then repeated. The distance may be increased to five yards for those with good technique.

2. Sit facing your partner with feet touching, arms out at the side. Throw the ball gently up towards your partner so that they come forward, bending at the waist, to head the ball firmly, but gently, back to their partner. Three headers, then change over.

3. Stand up five yards from your partner with one foot in front of the other. Throw the ball gently towards your partner above head height, so that leaning back, they bring their weight forward and head through the ball so that it reaches their partner without a bounce. Three headers, then change over.

As the players go through the above practices they will discover that heading different parts of the ball will produce different results.
> **If the midline of the ball or above is contacted, the ball will go down.**
> **If the point of contact is below the midline, the ball will rise.**

This information needs to be emphasised when practising the two main types of heading:

> Heading in defence.
> Heading in attack.

After the initial introduction, either of these techniques may be practised.

2) HEADING IN DEFENCE.

Mark Wright (England) leaps to head clear against Cameroon in the 1990 World Cup Quarter Final.

WHAT TO PRACTISE.

When players are defending, the most important thing is to clear the danger, gaining time for the defence to re-organise. This will be achieved from gaining height, width and distance.

In order to gain height, the ball must be contacted below the midline. Contacting underneath the ball will only send it straight up and although better than nothing, should be avoided.

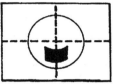

The ball should be headed wide so that if it does fall to an opponent, it will be in a less dangerous position and it is unlikely that a goal will be scored directly. Clearly, the more distance which can be gained, the further the ball will land from your goal and again, the less likely it is that a goal will be scored directly.

HOW TO PRACTISE.

1. In pairs about 5 yards apart facing eachother, one foot behind the other. Serve the ball to your partner, so he steps forward to head, directing the ball upwards to be caught above the head. This is achieved by contact below the mid line of the ball.
2. Starting five yards apart A1 serves high in front of B1, who runs forward and heads over A1. A1 turns, chases and stops the ball as quickly as possible. B1 runs after him and stops about five yards from A1. A1 serves again to B1 and the practice is repeated.

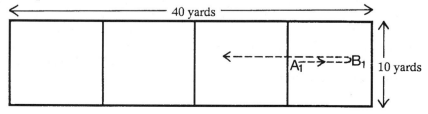

Count how many headers it takes B1 to reach the 40 yard gridline or whatever line is decided, according to the players' ability. B1 then serves to A1 on the way back to determine the winner - the player with the fewest headers. Emphasis should be placed on the quality of the service to enable the players to time their run and header.

3. In the diagram 'B' serves the ball high for 'A' to run forward and head over 'B' to 'C'. The quality of the service is important as 'A' must be able to time his run in relation to the flight of the ball. Rotate the position of the players every three headers. Players should now be encouraged to jump to head the ball and should use a one foot take-off.

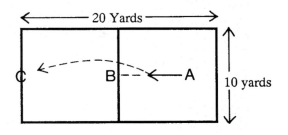

4. As above, but after serving, 'B' acts as a goalkeeper and tries to intercept headers made by both 'A' and 'C'. The headers should have height and power and the distances can be increased if necessary.

5. This practice is more advanced and takes place in a penalty area. A ball is served from S1, S2 or S3 and the defenders D1 and D2 must head clear. Calling should be encouraged and the goalkeeper must also play a full part in the practice, catching the ball if possible, rather than letting the defenders head it. Balls served from S1 and S3 should be directed to the opposite flank if possible. Balls from S2 may be headed to either S1 or S3. No header should bounce within the penalty area.

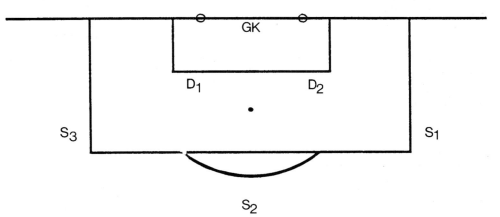

D1 and D2 should be encouraged to attack the ball and head it at its highest possible point, using a one foot take-off. Failure to do so in a game situation will allow opponents the chance to be first to the ball. This is not a pressure practice and time should be allowed for players to recover their positions.

6. An attacker A1 is added to the practice to provide opposition for D1 and D2.

7. Additional attackers and defenders can be added until the practice builds up to a realistic game situation.

3) HEADING IN ATTACK.

David Platt (England) scores with a downward header against Cameroon in the 1990 World Cup Quarter Final.

WHAT TO PRACTISE.

As with shooting, when players are heading for goal the most important factor is accuracy. Further, as with shooting, the most difficult ball for the goalkeeper to save will be low and just inside the post. It follows then, that when heading for goal this will be the main target area, provided the goalkeeper is well positioned.

The key factor will be to make contact with the midline of the ball or just above it.

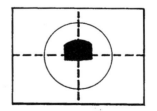

N.B. If for any reason the goalkeeper is badly positioned, then the target will obviously be the unguarded part of the goal. When the goalkeeper is too far off his line, it may be best to head the ball over him into an empty net. In such circumstances, the normal rule of heading the ball down may not apply.

HOW TO PRACTISE.

1. In pairs about five yards apart facing each other, one foot behind the other. Serve the ball to your partner so he steps forward to head, directing the ball downwards so that it bounces before reaching you. This is achieved by contact through the midline of the ball or slightly above it.

2. Once the above technique is satisfactory the ball may be served slightly higher so that the players have to jump to get above the ball and head it down, using the neck and trunk muscles. A one foot take-off is required.

3. Make five yard goals and with players 10 yards apart, try to score by heading the ball past your partner. Aim for the corner of the goal and try to make the ball bounce before it crosses the line. The ball is served from the hands and any return headers from the server which score, count double. Three headers then change over.

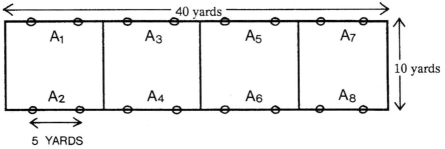

4. In fours in a ten yard grid with a goalkeeper, an attacker, a server and a retriever. The goal is full size. S1 serves to A1 who runs in and heads for goal. 'R' acts as a retriever and returns the ball to S1. Rotate the positions frequently. The position from which the ball is served (S1, S2, S3) can be varied from session to session, so that different technique may be required (eg. deflections).

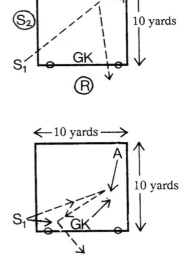

5. If the goalkeeper is positioned to prevent a goal at the near post, A1 may head back across goal where S1 can become a second attacker and if necessary, finish off the move.

6. This practice is more advanced and takes place in the penalty area with two servers, two attackers and a goalkeeper. The ball is served from alternate sides and A1 and A2 must try and score with a header. The ball may be played to both the near and far post. If either attacker does not think he can score, the ball may be headed to the other player to finish off the move. Calling should be encouraged between the attacking players. The attackers should also be encouraged to attack the ball and be first to it, jumping or diving to meet it as early as possible. There will be ample opportunity for the practice of diving headers.

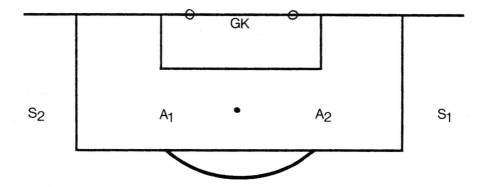

7. A defender D1 is added to provide opposition for A1 and A2.
8. Additional players may be introduced gradually to increase the realism and build up to a game situation.

NB. In practice situations like this, care should again be taken to avoid clashes of heads leading to serious injuries.

4. DEFLECTION HEADING.

Most attacking and defensive headers direct the ball within 90 degrees of where the ball came from.

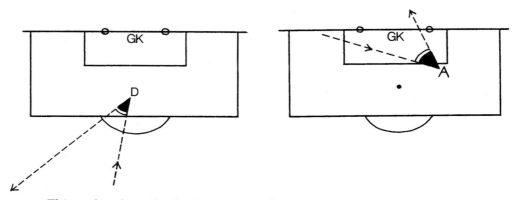

This makes the task of gaining power far easier, although such headers are also easier to predict. Far less easy to predict and therefore of great use when attacking, are deflection headers. Deflection headers use the pace of the ball, but alter the line of its flight. They are of two main types:

        A)   Deflections to the side.
        B)   Deflections backwards.

A. DEFLECTIONS TO THE SIDE.

These are usually used when attacking players are heading for goal or to other colleagues through angles greater than 90 degrees. The technique requires the head to be turned at the moment of impact in order to change the direction of the ball. The point of contact is still the forehead, although not necessarily the centre part. The other key factors are the same as for the two types of heading already discussed. The advantage of deflection heading to the side is that it is almost impossible to predict the flight of the ball, but it is difficult to get a good contact, as timing the turn of the head is difficult. This technique requires much practice.

B. DEFLECTIONS BACKWARDS.

This technique is most effective when used by an attacking player who has his back to goal.

(i) In a central position, the ball may be flicked on behind the defence for a team-mate to run on to.

(ii) In a position short of the near post the ball may be flicked on towards the back post with devastating effect. As with deflections to the side, the flight of the ball is difficult to predict, but again this is an advanced technique which requires much practice.

Claudio Caniggia (Argentina) deflects the ball backwards past Zenga and Ferri (Italy) to score in the 1990 World Cup Quarter Final.

WHAT TO PRACTISE.

The technique is almost the opposite to orthodox heading, in that the head moves backward on impact, helping the ball on its way. The flick of the head results in an arched position of the body.

The point of contact is the top part of the forehead where the hairline starts. The more delicate the contact is, the less the ball will be deflected. For maximum effect the pace of the ball should be maintained or preferably increased, as this will give opponents less time to react.

Before contact.　　　　　After contact.

HOW TO PRACTISE.

1. In threes, five yards apart. 'B' and 'C' face 'A' who serves to 'B' fairly quickly, but above head height. 'B' flicks the ball to 'C' and the practice then starts from 'C'. Change the players' positions frequently.

2. When the technique is satisfactory, increase the distance between the players to ten yards and increase the pace of the service.

3. This practice takes place in one end of the pitch where S1 and S2 are servers, alternately delivering corners to A1 and A2 respectively. The corners should ideally be in-swingers. A1 and A2 try to flick the ball on to each other, eliminating the goalkeeper from catching the ball. A1 and A2 should start at the near post but move towards the ball, adjusting their run as necessary. The servers S1 and S2 should concentrate on delivering the ball in an area short of the near post to prevent the goalkeeper having an easy catch of the ball.

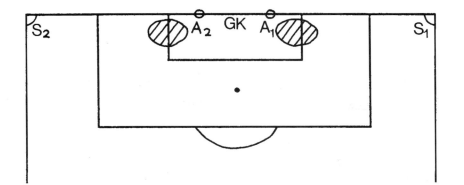

4. The above practice can be developed by introducing extra defenders and attackers to produce a realistic match situation. This practice is good both for attacking corners, as well as for heightening defensive awareness in countering such moves.

5. DIVING HEADERS.

One of the most spectacular aspects of Association Football is the diving header, most often seen in and around the penalty area. It is sometimes used by defenders in a desperate attempt to clear the ball, but it is more commonly used by attackers when trying to score. Provided the ground is soft, diving headers can be practised just like any other technique and indeed, can be great fun!

WHAT TO PRACTISE.
The four points given under the introduction to heading (p.69) also apply to diving headers. In addition, the following apply:
1. The ball must be served well away from the player (2-3 yards).
2. The player should throw himself at the ball, using his arms for momentum.
3. The arms are held out to give balance in flight and to help with landing.
4. It is vital that the head is held up throughout, so that the ball can be watched until the moment of contact.

After contact. (Note the head is up and that the arms are ready to help absorb the impact of landing.)

HOW TO PRACTISE.

1. Players work in pairs 5 yards apart facing eachother. A1 serves the ball in front of A2 who dives forward to head the ball back for A1 to catch. Three headers then change over.

2. As above, but the server indicates where the ball should be headed by holding a hand out, either right, left or above the head. This should be done as soon as the ball has been served.

3. Players work in threes in a triangle 5 yards apart. A1 serves for A2 to head to A3, who then becomes the server. After ten headers, reverse the direction of the service.

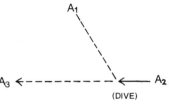

4. In groups of four in a 10 yard grid ,with 8 yard goals on all sides. A1 starts with the ball and serves to any of the other three players for a diving header. The player may head for any goal, depending on the service.The first player to total 5 goals or clean saves, is the winner. When a goal is scored, or the ball is saved, the practice starts again.

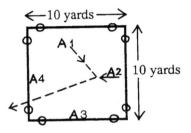

5. In a penalty area, pairs of attackers try to score using diving headers. The ball is served from close to the goal line from alternate sides. Services must have a low trajectory, forcing the attackers to use diving headers. The player not heading should be alert to secondary chances from the ball going across goal, or coming back from the post, crossbar or goalkeeper.

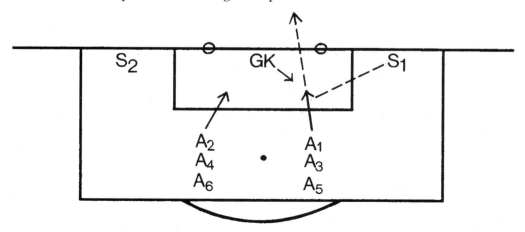

6. DEFENDING.

Without possession of the ball, no team will be able to attack their opponents or score goals. Clearly, it is very important that all players know and understand the best ways of preventing their opponents scoring and of gaining possession of the ball.

Although most of the other techniques in this book relate to situations when you are already in possession of the ball, the exceptions are goalkeeping and defending. To be exact, a technique can only be performed when you come into contact with the ball. Major parts of goalkeeping and defending involve making decisions to put you in the best position to either secure possession, or to deny your opponents the opportunity to take advantage of the possession they have.

The only technique involved in defending is tackling, which is only a small part of the whole topic of defending. In normal circumstances, 3 main tackles are used:

(i) The front block tackle.

As its name suggests, the aim of this tackle is to block the ball when facing your opponent. The inside of the foot is used as this offers a large area and the ankle is kept firm. The non-kicking foot is placed as close to the ball as possible and the body should be over the ball, to provide good balance and transfer the tackler's weight through the ball. The tackler should only block the ball and not try to kick it away.

(ii) The side block tackle.

This is very similar to the front block tackle and all the points are the same except that the challenge is made from the side.

(iii) The sliding tackle.

Although the sliding tackle is perhaps spectacular, it is a sure sign that the opposition have momentarily gained the upper hand. When defending, no player should choose to make a sliding tackle, except in an emergency. This is because the player attempting the tackle will be on the ground for a few seconds and out of the game. The sliding tackle is therefore best used near to the touchline or goal line, where the ball can be put out of play, allowing the defender time to recover. It may also be used to play the ball away from an attacker to the goalkeeper or a team-mate, when the challenging defender is unable to get in a position goalside of the ball.

The sliding tackle is almost always made from slightly behind the attacking player, which increases the chances of the defender committing a foul. Either foot may be used to play the ball, although most players tend to use their preferred one. The furthest foot offers a stronger tackling position, but the nearest one requires less time to play the ball. Whenever possible, the defender should try to get goalside of his opponent, rather than making a sliding tackle.

The majority of defending involves making decisions about how to adopt the best position to prevent your opponent from attacking you. Once a player has mastered those decision-making processes, all that remains is the fairly simple task of playing the ball away, either out of play or to a team-mate, or taking possession of it himself. The key to the latter is in correctly anticipating the opponent's next move and in reacting quickly to the situation. Naturally, if possible, the ball should be intercepted before it reaches the opponent, but the defender's priority should be to remain goalside - if a defender is overconcerned with making interceptions, he will adopt poor defensive positions and place his team at risk. Interceptions are most common when the ball is underhit and the receiving player does not meet the ball.

When challenging for a loose ball, it is essential that the defender tries to get his body between the opponent and the ball, which will not only give him time, but also make it very difficult for the opponent to win possession without committing a foul and conceding a free kick.

With regard to decision-making, a defender's task will come under 3 main headings:

     1) Preventing opponents turning.
     2) Preventing opponents playing the ball forward.
     3) Forcing play into certain areas.

1. PREVENTING OPPONENTS TURNING.

Usually players who have their back to their opponent's goal present the least threat as they are unable to pass, dribble or shoot the ball forward without first turning. If opponents can be kept in positions with their backs to goal, this should bring the maximum advantage to the defending team. In order to achieve this, at the moment the attacker receives the ball, it is essential that the defender adopts the correct defensive position.

WHAT TO PRACTISE.

1. When marking an opponent with his back to goal not in possession of the ball, the defender should be on a line from the opponent to the centre of his own goal. He should be able to see the ball and his opponent from a distance where, if the ball is played to the opponent, the defender can make up the ground to be in a position about 2-3 feet behind the opponent when he receives it, to prevent him from turning.

   The starting distance will depend on how far away the ball is and the speed of the defender. The nearer the ball and the slower the defender, the closer must be the starting position. If the ball is 50-60 yards away and the defender is quick, it may be possible to start some 10 yards away from your opponent and still make the ground up if the ball is played to your opponent. The added advantage of this is that by occupying a less tight marking position, the opposition are discouraged from playing the ball into the space behind you.

2. As the ball is played to your opponent, the defender must quickly make up ground as the ball travels. If the ball is played closer to your opponent, but not directly to him, the defender should move closer, but not as tight as if the opponent had possession of the ball.

3. As the opponent receives the ball, the defender should check his advance and ideally be 2-3 feet behind his opponent. If he is further away, he should observe the quality and direction of the opponent's first touch, before deciding whether to continue to advance or not.

4. When the defender stops advancing, he should adopt a balanced stance, on his toes, with feet apart, one in front of the other. The balanced position means he will be able to move in any direction to counter the opponent's next move.

5. The defender must continually watch the ball and maintain a position between it and his own goal. If the opponent moves the ball in any direction, the defender must react to it and move so that he can at all times prevent his opponent from turning. If the defender gets too close to the opponent, he will not be able to see the ball.

6. At this stage, it is not the defender's task to try and win the ball and he should remain patient and stay on his feet. The attacker has the main problem, not the defender.

7. If the opponent miscontrols the ball, or plays it where the defender can reach it, he should challenge for the ball and try to win it. Otherwise, the defender should only try to win the ball when the opponent tries to turn. It is vital therefore, that the defender 'shadows' his opponent, so that if he does try to turn, he is close enough to make a challenge - i.e. 2-3 feet away.

Tony Dorigo (Leeds United) tries to prevent Dwight Yorke (Aston Villa) from turning with the ball. Dorigo is watching the ball carefully, but Yorke has cleverly backed into him to locate the defender's position and to obscure his view of the ball.

HOW TO PRACTISE.

1. In an area 30 yards X 10 yards, S1 passes to A1, who must try to turn and pass to S2. As the ball travels to A1, D1 makes up the ground and tries to prevent A1 from turning with the ball. D1 should start in a position between A1 and S2, at a distance of about 2-3 yards.

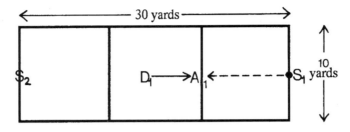

2. Whether D1 is successful or not, the next part of the practice starts with the ball served from S2. This time A1 and D1 reverse roles, with D1 now becoming the attacker and A1 the defender.
3. S1 and S2 change with D1 and D2 every ten services, so that all players get a chance to act as defenders.
4. Once competent in the above situations, players should then be given the opportunity to practise their defending in small-sided games.

2. PREVENTING OPPONENTS PLAYING THE BALL FORWARD.

In some instances, it will not be possible to prevent opponents from turning with the ball. This might be because the opponent has received the ball in space and has already turned, or because poor defending has allowed him to turn. In either case, the best must be made of the situation, which means the defender should now try to stop the opponent from playing the ball forward. When the ball is allowed to be played forward, a large threat is posed and so this should be prevented whenever possible.

WHAT TO PRACTISE.

1. When a defender is facing an opponent in possession, the distance between them is a vital factor. Many defenders are reluctant to get close because they think they may be hit with the ball. It is, however, far more dangerous to stay back, as the further away the defender is, the more chance there is that the opponent will try and play the ball past him and that it will be lifted off the ground. The best distance is 1-2 yards. The defender's first objective should be to get in line between his opponent and the target. Once he is in line, then he can move down the line towards his opponent.
2. The defender should make up the ground as the ball is travelling to his opponent as quickly as possible. Once the opponent has control of the ball, the defender, if not already within the optimum 1-2 yards, should slow the speed of his approach.

If he does not, the opponent will find it easy to throw him off balance and play the ball past him. The defender should still try to close the distance between him and the opponent, by edging slowly towards him in a balanced position.

3. The defender should stay between the ball and the target, watching the ball all the time.

4. By getting close, the defender will force the opponent to have his head down, so that he cannot fully weigh up the attacking possibilities. The defender can try to gain the initiative by pretending to tackle for the ball. Such a movement may be enough to panic the opponent, making him lose control of the ball and presenting the defender with an opportunity to win it.

5. The defender should be patient and stay on his feet. The longer the opponent has the ball, the more time there is for the defender's team-mates to adopt good covering positions.

Stuart Pearce (England) prevents Thomas Berthold (West Germany) from playing the ball forward during the 1990 World Cup Semi-Final.
(Note Pearce's half-turned position.)

HOW TO PRACTISE.

1. In an area 20 yards X 10 yards, S1 passes along the ground to A1, who must pass back to S1. As soon as S1 passes, D1 moves into the line of the pass and then down the line towards A1. D1 moving into the line of the pass will discourage A1 from passing first time and give D1 time to challenge. If he can, D1 should intercept the pass and his movement, until A1 touches the ball, should be as quick as possible.

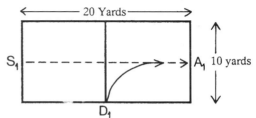

2. Once the practise is finished, A1 and S1 change roles, with the ball served from the opposite end and D2 becoming the defender.
3. After ten services A1 and S1 change with D1 and D2, so that all players have the opportunity to practise defending.
4. The side of the grid from which the defender approaches should also be varied to give experience of differing lines of approach.
5. To make it more difficult, the distance from which D1 has to run can be increased to 15 yards.
6. Once competent in the above situations, players should be given the opportunity to practise their defending in small-sided games.

3. FORCING PLAY INTO CERTAIN AREAS.

If an opponent has already turned, the defenders can make the most of the situation by encouraging him to travel or play the ball into areas where there is either less threat to the defence, or where defenders have a numerical advantage, or preferably both. Similarly, if the opponent can be encouraged to play the ball to a teammate who has his back to goal, this will give the initiative back, in part, to the defending team. This can be achieved by those defenders goalside of the ball dropping off their immediate opponent to discourage the ball from being played behind them. They should only drop off to a distance from which, if the ball is played to their opponent, they can make up the ground and prevent him from turning.

The 2 main areas into which play might be forced to the advantage of the defending team are:

        (I)   Near the touchline.
        (II)   Across the field.

N.B. Of course, forcing play into either area will have no advantage to the defending team if the defenders are poor at the individual aspects of defending.

(I) NEAR THE TOUCHLINE.

When play is forced into areas near the touchline, this can have several advantages for the defending team:

        a) The attacker will have less space in which to manoevre.
        b) The attacker will have less passing options.
        c) The attacker will have less of an angle through which to pass the ball.
        d) The defenders may be able to isolate the attacker.

WHAT TO PRACTISE.
A) THE CHALLENGING PLAYER.
1. In order to force play into areas near the touchline, the challenging defender should position himself so that the opponent with the ball is blocked from going across the field and is offered the angle to move only in the defender's preferred direction.

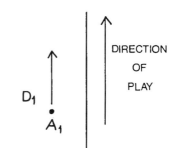

2. The defender should adopt a half-turned position, facing the touchline with feet parallel to it, so that he can recover quickly if the ball is played past him.
3. The defender should be in a low position, well-balanced and on the balls of his feet.
4. The defender should be no more than 2 yards from the ball, otherwise the opponent will be able to look up and play the ball past him.
5. The defender should watch the ball.

Paul Gascoigne (England) forces Lothar Matthaeus (West Germany) down the touchline and towards the covering defender Stuart Pearce in the 1990 World Cup Semi-Final.

B) THE COVERING PLAYER.

1. The correct supporting position is one that allows the covering player the best chance of challenging for the ball, irrespective of whether D1 is beaten on the inside or on the outside. Because the greatest danger will probably come on the outside, as the attacker is being forced that way, the covering player should favour that side. This position allows D2 to see both A1 and the ball.

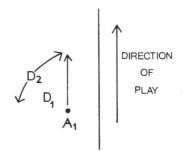

2. It is important that D2 communicates with D1, giving him both encouragement and information about both of their positions. This will assist the challenging player in deciding whether to try and win the ball and, if so, when.
3. The most important question for the covering player is "how far behind the challenging player should he position himself?" This is difficult to answer, but the player should be close enough to challenge the opponent before he can regain

possession after beating D1, but far enough away to prevent the opponent playing the ball past both defenders and regaining possession.

The chances of the opponent doing either of these will have to be assessed according to four factors:

(i) The skill of the opponent.

If, the opponent has good dribbling skills, the covering player may need to be in a close supporting position.

(ii) The defensive qualities of the challenging player.

If the challenging player is a good defender, the covering player will be able to support from further back.

(iii) The comparative speeds of the covering player and his opponent.

If the speed advantage is with the opponent, the covering player must adopt a deep position. If the advantage is with the covering player, he will be able to move in a closer covering position.

(iv) The area of the field.

In and around the penalty area, it is unlikely that the ball can be played easily past both defenders, so a close covering position should be adopted to prevent shots or crosses. In other areas of the field, there may be more space to be exploited behind the covering defender and so a deeper covering position can be used.

N.B. As a rough guide, it is recommended that close covering positions should be 2-4 yards behind the challenging player. Deep covering positions should be 5-8 yards behind the challenging player.

As one Finnish defender challenges Lineker (England) to prevent him from turning, his team-mate adopts a close covering position during a 1992 International match.

HOW TO PRACTISE.

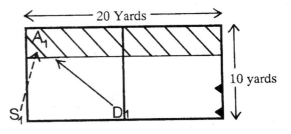

1. In an area 20 yards X 10 yards, S1 passes the ball to A1, who must try to dribble between the cones. As the ball travels to A1, D1 moves to challenge and adopts a position to force A1 down the shaded area, reducing the angle for A1 to dribble between the cones. D1 should win the ball if he has the chance.

2. Every 10 services, the players should rotate positions, so that they all get a chance to act as the defender.

3. The area is now increased to 30 yards X 10 yards and an extra defender is introduced. As the ball travels from 'S' to A1, D2 must now move to support D1. D2 must cover D1 and challenge for the ball if D1 is beaten. It is important that D1 adopts the correct challenging position and that D2 assumes the correct supporting position.

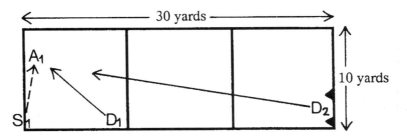

4. In the same area 'S' now becomes a second attacker (A2), initially creating a 2 V 1 situation. D2 must combine with D1 to prevent the attackers reaching the end of the grid area. The cones are now removed and the offside rule applies.

(II) ACROSS THE FIELD.

When play is forced across the field, this can have four main advantages for the defending team:

(i)   The opponent's progress towards goal is halted.
(ii) The play is kept in front of the defence.
(iii) Recovering players have more time to get goalside of the ball.
(iv) Recovering players may have the chance of challenging for the ball as they make their recovery runs.

N.B. It is vital that when a player is forced across the field, pressure should be maintained otherwise he may turn up the field and threaten the defence by passing the ball forward, or shooting.

WHAT TO PRACTISE.
A) THE CHALLENGING PLAYER.

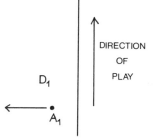

1. In order to force play across the field, the challenging defender should position himself so that the opponent with the ball is blocked from going down the line and is offered the angle to move only in the defender's preferred direction.
2. The defender should adopt a half-turned position, facing infield, with feet parallel to the touchline, so that he can recover quickly if the ball is played past him.
3. The defender should be in a low position, well-balanced and on the balls of his feet.
4. The defender should be no more than 2 yards from the ball, otherwise the opponent will be able to look up and play the ball past him.

B) THE COVERING PLAYER.

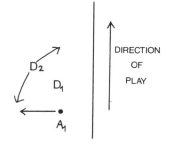

1. The correct supporting position is one that allows the covering player the best chance of challenging for the ball, irrespective of whether D1 is beaten on the inside or the outside. Because the greatest danger will probably come on the inside, as the attacker is being forced that way, the covering player should favour that side. This position allows D2 to see both A1 and the ball.
2. It is important that D2 communicates with D1, giving him both encouragement and information about both of their positions. This will assist the challenging player in deciding whether to try and win the ball and, if so, when.
3. The considerations as discussed in B (p.85), are all relevant to this situation, the only difference being that the immediate danger is usually somewhat less, as the opponent is moving across the field, rather than forward.

As the first Polish defender forces Barnes (England) across the field, the second defender moves up to maintain the pressure, making Barnes play the ball back.

HOW TO PRACTISE.

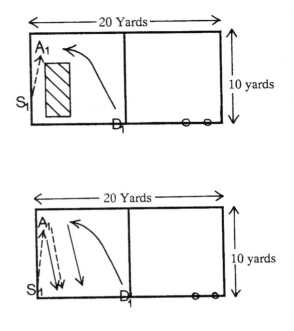

1. In an area 20 yards X 10 yards, S1 passes the ball to A1, who must try to dribble between the cones. As the ball travels to A1, D1 moves to challenge and adopts a position to force A1 across the field into the shaded area, reducing the angle for A1 to dribble beween the cones. D1 should win the ball if he has the chance.

2. If A1 is successfully manoeuvred into the shaded area, D1 must move across and quickly pressurise, preventing A1 from moving forward. This movement should be slightly angled backwards, to discourage A1 from playing the ball into the space behind D1. The situation should then be repeated, this time with D1 forcing A1 across the field to the right. Thus, unless he wins the ball, D1 will retreat slowly in a series of zig-zags, preventing A1 from making quick forward progress.

3. Every 10 services, the players should rotate positions, so that they all have a chance of acting as defenders.

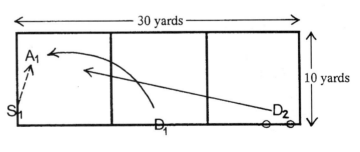

4. The area is now increased to 30 yards X 10 yards and an extra defender is introduced. As the ball travels from S to A1, D2 must now move to support D1. D2 must cover D1 and challenge for the ball if D1 is beaten. It is important that D1 adopts the correct challenging position and that D2 assumes the correct supporting position.

5. The organisation is the same as above, except that when the ball is served, D2 must make a recovery run from a cone 5 yards behind the server's grid line. D2 may challenge for the ball whilst making the recovery run, or move behind D1 to cover him, depending on the situation.

6. As above initially, but 'S' now becomes a second attacker (A2), creating a 2 V 1 situation. D1 must force the attackers to play the ball across the field, allowing D2 time to recover. D2 must count to 3 seconds (later 5), before he can start his recovery run. D1 and D2 then combine to try and prevent A1 and A2 from reaching the end of the 30 yard area. The offside rule should apply. Change defender's roles every 5 services and attackers with defenders every 10 services.

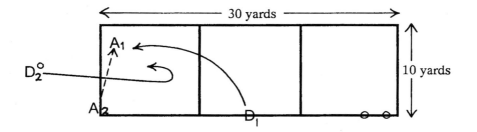

7. GOALKEEPING.

The results of many matches are decided by the comparative quality of the two goalkeepers. It follows, therefore, that a great deal of time should be spent improving and maintaining the techniques of goalkeepers. Unfortunately, even more than outfield players, good goalkeepers rely a great deal on making correct decisions, as well as on good technique. Some of those decisions are discussed here, but owing to limitations of space, others, particularly relating to dealing with crosses, are not.

Goalkeeping is often neglected in coaching, perhaps because it is such a specialist position that few coaches feel adept at dealing with players who may be more knowledgeable than themselves. This should not be allowed to happen and with basic information at their fingertips, all coaches should become involved in this vital aspect of the game.

The first principle which should be understood is that the goalkeeper has an enormous advantage over the rest of the players in the use of his hands. This advantage is not always fully understood. Once the goalkeeper gains full possession of the ball, unlike outfield players, provided he takes adequate care, he cannot legally be dispossessed. He can therefore exert a controlling influence on the game, more so than any other player. Provided this does not incorporate time wasting, it can be of great benefit to a team.

For a goalkeeper to have any influence on a game, he must first be able to control the ball. For a goalkeeper, the principles of controlling the ball are identical to those for any other player, except of course goalkeepers will almost always use their hands. Because of the immediate danger of conceding a goal, it is vital that goalkeepers try to get their body behind the ball and catch it as early as possible. As the ball may sometimes not be held at the first attempt, goalkeepers should always be alert and ready to make a second attempt to secure the ball or to make a second save.

A. GETTING YOUR BODY BEHIND THE BALL.

Having your body behind the ball provides a second line of defence should the hands fail to stop it. For catching balls above head height or when there is not enough time to get the body behind the ball, then the hands will be the only means of stopping the ball. Correct technique is therefore vital.

B. CATCHING THE BALL AS EARLY AS POSSIBLE.

With the likelihood of there being attackers nearby, it is always safest to catch the ball as early as possible, to prevent opponents getting to the ball first. When the ball is below head height, the goalkeeper should move down the line of flight as far as he can. When the ball is above head height, the goalkeeper should catch it at the highest point within his reach.

Before considering different goalkeeping techniques for catching the ball, consideration must first be given to the position the goalkeeper should adopt in preparation for making a save. This position is known as 'the ready position' and should be adopted when the attacking player draws his leg back to shoot, or attempts to dribble the ball past the goalkeeper.

1. THE READY POSITION.

WHAT TO PRACTISE.
In the ready position, the goalkeeper should concentrate on the following:
1. Feet shoulder width apart, weight forward.
2. Knees slightly bent, ready to move in any direction.
3. Head slightly forward, steady and with the eyes on the ball.
4. Hands at waist height, outside the line of the body, palms facing the ball, fingers straight.
5. Relaxed, but ready.

N.B. At no time, apart from a penalty kick should a goalkeeper adopt this position when standing on his goal line - he should always be in front of it, the distance being dependent on where the ball is. (See p.102). This provides a safety margin in case the ball is only partly stopped when making a save.

The Ready Position.

HOW TO PRACTISE.
1. Check the ready position of the goalkeeper when gently shooting in from the edge of the penalty area. Introduce the above key factors as necessary.
2. Repeat the above, playing the ball gently forward right or left into the penalty area for a player to chase and shoot. Check the goalkeeper's position when the attacker's foot is drawn back to shoot. Re-coach as necessary.
3. Using any kind of shooting or crossing practice, check the goalkeeper's position prior to delivery of the ball. In matches or game situations, re-check the goalkeeper's ready position. Re-trace the above practices as necessary.

2. CATCHING THE BALL ABOVE HEAD HEIGHT.

As already mentioned, a goalkeeper should catch the ball at as high a point as possible. This avoids the possibility of opponents getting to the ball first.

WHAT TO PRACTISE.
1. The goalkeeper should assess the line of flight of the ball and move to intercept it at the maximum comfortable height, preferably with a jump. This has the added advantage of usually taking him away from the area where opponents and team-mates may also be jumping to head the ball.

2. To gain maximum height, the take-off should be one-footed. This also gives protection to the goalkeeper.

3. Whenever possible, the ball should be caught above and in front of the head, so that it is in the line of vision and late adjustments may be made if necessary.

4. The fingers should be spread and relaxed, helping the forearms to absorb the impact of the ball on contact.

5. The hands should be close together, behind and to the side of the ball. Notice the 'W' shape made by the thumbs and first fingers.

6. Once the ball is caught, it should be brought into the body immediately, to prevent it from being knocked loose. A goalkeeper may use what-ever method is comfortable, but it should not involve the arms moving outside the line of the body. Usu-ally, the dominant hand turns the ball as it is brought down and the other hand slides round it, so the ball is held firmly to the chest by both hands and forearms.

HOW TO PRACTISE.

1. The practice takes place in a penalty area, or any area 20 yards by 10 yards, with full size goals. Initially, the ball is thrown by the server directly to the goalkeeper, so that it is caught above head height. The key points outlined above should be observed.

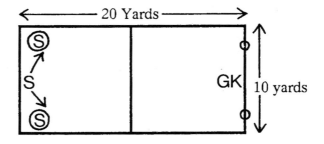

2. The practice may be developed by the server kicking the ball directly to the goalkeeper, or in front of him, so that he must move forward to catch it.

3. Once the goalkeeper shows satisfactory technique, the ball is then thrown slightly to the right or left of the goalkeeper, so that a sideways movement is required.

4. The server may kick the ball slightly to the right or left of the goalkeeper.

5. Finally, a variety of services are kicked at the goalkeeper. This should include balls served from wide angles and therefore a larger practice area will be required. This should create instances where the goalkeeper has to move backwards to catch, as well as forwards and sideways.

6. One team-mate may now be introduced to work in conjunction with the goalkeeper and clear, early calling should now be emphasised.

7. An opponent may now be introduced to challenge for the ball.

8. Additional team-mates and opponents may be introduced to create a match-like situation.

3. CATCHING THE BALL AT CHEST HEIGHT.

WHAT TO PRACTISE.
There are two main techniques which can be used:
A)   Cupping/scooping.
B)   Catching.

A. CUPPING/SCOOPING.
With this method, the ball is allowed to hit the chest and at the same time the hands come upward and around the ball, cupping it against the chest. At the moment of impact the body curls, thus absorbing some of the pace of the ball. The head should be steady and the eyes watch the ball.

B. CATCHING.
This technique is very similar to catching balls above head height, except that the hands reach out in front of the body to provide a cushioning space. Again, the head must be steady with the eyes on the ball.

A. Cupping / Scooping.

B. Catching.

HOW TO PRACTISE.
(The organisation for the practice is identical to that in 2 above.)
1. Balls are first thrown straight to the goalkeeper at chest height. Note the techniques as detailed above, including the ready position.
2. If satisfactory, balls may be kicked straight at the goalkeeper.
3. Balls are then thrown two to three yards either side of the goalkeeper, who should use a side-stepping action to get his body behind the line of the ball. The feet should click together and not cross over each other. Note the technique for catching the ball.
4. Kick the ball two to three yards either side of the goalkeeper and note the techniques detailed above.
5. In a game situation observe the technique of the goalkeeper and if necessary return to the above practices as appropriate.

4. CATCHING THE BALL AT WAIST HEIGHT AND BELOW.

WHAT TO PRACTISE.

The cupping/scooping technique as detailed in 3 above is normally used, with the ball brought into the waist. When the ball is below waist height, the legs buckle together under the body, which falls forward allowing the hands to come under the ball. The leg should provide a second barrier to the ball if the hands fail to stop it. A half kneeling technique may also be used, particularly when the ball has bounced in front of the goalkeeper. This bending of the knees lowers the body and brings the hands behind the line of the ball. The hands take the pace off the ball by catching it slightly away from the thighs. The ball is then secured to the chest.

The legs have buckled under the body, allowing the hands to come under the ball.

The ball being scooped up into the body, using the half-kneeling technique.

HOW TO PRACTISE.

The organisation and progressions for the above practice are identical to those in 2 above, except that the ball is served at waist height and below.

5. TAKING THE BALL ALONG THE GROUND.

WHAT TO PRACTISE.
Two main techniques are used: A) Stooping. B) Kneeling.

A. STOOPING
This technique is often used on flat surfaces when the ball is rolling fairly gently. The goalkeeper gets behind the line of the ball and bends forward at the waist, allowing the hands to reach forward and stop the ball. The legs are slightly bent and close together, providing a second barrier to the ball if the hands fail to stop it. The head should be steady and the eyes watching the ball. The ball may be stopped to allow the goalkeeper to play it again, or it may be scooped up to the chest.

B. KNEELING
On poor surfaces, or when the ball is travelling hard or bouncing, it is safer to get your whole body behind the ball. On such occasions the kneeling technique is used. Having got behind the line of the ball, the goalkeeper goes down on one knee placing it close to , but in front of the other foot, to prevent the ball going through should the hands miss it. The feet point sideways, but the body is turned so that the head and chest are facing the ball. The hands are close together, with fingers spread and reach out to scoop the ball into the chest. The head is steady and the eyes watch the ball. When the goalkeeper moves to the side, he should go down on the opposite knee. i.e. When moving right, go down on the left knee.

A. Stooping.

B. Kneeling.

HOW TO PRACTISE.
The organisation and progressions are identical to those for 2 above, except that the ball is played along the ground.

6. DIVING.

Only when the goalkeeper does not have time to get his body behind the ball as a second line of defence, or when the ball is struck low and hard at him, should he need to dive. A goalkeeper should only dive when absolutely necessary.

A. SHOTS CLOSE TO THE BODY.

WHAT TO PRACTISE.

Diving is necessary in cases where the ball has considerable pace. Where the ball is low and straight at the goalkeeper, he must get down quickly to ensure his body is behind the ball. One method is to quickly move both legs out to one side. Having removed the support, the body collapses behind the line of the ball. The hands move to the ball and secure it with one hand behind and the other on top, before bringing it into the body.

A second method is to bend one knee under the body whilst the other leg moves out to the side. Again, the hands secure the ball and bring it into the body. This method is likely to be used for low shots slightly to the side of the body.

The buckling save for shots slightly to the side of the body. Note that the hands are leading.

HOW TO PRACTISE.

1. Serve the ball from about five yards. Roll it hard along the ground, straight at the goalkeeper. Check the goalkeeper's ready position and his ability to quickly throw his legs out of the way and get his body behind the ball. The hands should immediately move behind the line of the ball. Note the technique for stopping the ball and securing it to the body.
2. Move to about ten yards away and kick the ball low and hard at the goalkeeper. Re-check the technique already mentioned.
3. Introduce the technique of bending the knee under the body for those shots slightly to the side of the goalkeeper. Check the technique, hand position and securing procedure. With varied service, observe the goalkeeper's choice of technique according to the situation.
4. Introduce an attacking player to follow up for rebounds which the goalkeeper has failed to hold.

B. SHOTS WIDE OF THE BODY.

WHAT TO PRACTISE.

With shots wide of the body, the goalkeeper may need to dive long distances. To do so, he must thrust off with the foot nearest to the ball, so he must bend that leg before take-off. This will help maintain the sideways-on position, enabling him to see the ball throughout its flight. The hands and fingers are in the same position as when catching a high ball above the head. Once caught, the ball may be brought into the body in mid-air or after landing. If the latter is chosen, to avoid the ball being knocked loose on landing, some goalkeepers twist in mid-air in order to place the ball on the ground, before they themselves land. This is an extremely advanced technique. For shots on the ground, the lower hand is spread behind the ball and the upper hand comes down to trap the ball against the ground, before securing it to the body.

Having caught the ball in a sideways-on position, the hands begin to bring it into the body before landing.

HOW TO PRACTISE

1. From about five yards, with the goalkeeper kneeling on the ground, throw the ball wide of him, but close enough to reach. Check the goalkeeper maintains a sideways-on position throughout the dive and check the catching and securing technique. Serve to alternate sides at first, then at random to either side. Allow an adequate rest period.
2. From the same distance, with the goalkeeper now standing up, throw the ball wide of him, as above. In addition to the points already made, check the take-off technique. To increase the distance the goalkeeper is able to reach, a low obstacle such as a sports bag full of bibs may be placed 6" to 1' to the side of the goalkeeper. This will encourage him to thrust upwards and achieve greater distance when he dives.
3. Finally, check the technique for securing the ball, either before or after landing.
4. Increase the distance to 10 to 15 yards and re-check all the above. This time the ball should be kicked by the server, just inside the corner of the goal.
5. Introduce an attacking player to follow up for rebounds which the goalkeeper has failed to hold.
6. Observe the technique of the goalkeeper in match situations and return to the above practice situations as appropriate.

7. DEFLECTING THE BALL.

When a goalkeeper deflects the ball, it should preferably go round the post or over the bar. The reason for this is obvious - a ball which is deflected, but remains in play, may fall to an opponent in a position from which a goal may be scored.

A. DEFLECTING OVER THE BAR.

1. SHOTS TO THE SIDE OF THE GOALKEEPER.

WHAT TO PRACTISE.

In this situation it is usual for one hand to be used - the one nearest to the ball - although some goalkeepers wrongly use their preferred hand, no matter which side the ball is. Take-off is important and a good upward thrust from the nearest leg will assist. The ball should be deflected with the open palm of the hand and firm fingers, giving a large area of contact on the ball. Not too much pace should be taken out of the ball or it may drop into the open goal, or fall in a dangerous area.

HOW TO PRACTISE.

1. Initially, the goalkeeper should start 2 to 3 yards off his line and the ball be thrown from 12 to 15 yards. The throw must be hard and high, slightly to the side of the goalkeeper, otherwise deflecting should not be necessary. Check the ready position and the ability to thrust off, as well as the technique of deflecting. Serve to alternate sides and allow rest periods.

2. Increase the distance that the ball is served wide of the goalkeeper. Assess the goal keeper's ability to thrust off and reach the ball.

3. Serve to either side at random.

4. Now kick the ball by dropping and volleying it, varying the pace and distance away from the goalkeeper.

5. Observe the goalkeeper in match situations and return to the above practices as appropriate.

2. SHOTS OVER THE HEAD OF THE GOALKEEPER.

WHAT TO PRACTISE.

If the goalkeeper is off his line and the ball is played over him, he should get back as quickly as possible to try and make a save. The goalkeeper should not turn, but move backwards so that he is able to watch the ball all of the time. When moving backwards, it is dangerous to attempt a catch, therefore the ball should be helped over the bar. When the ball is sufficiently low to reach, the goalkeeper should turn his body, helping the ball over the bar with the hand nearest the field of play. The hand should be open and the palm upwards. This turning action helps protect the goalkeeper from opponents who may be challenging him.

HOW TO PRACTISE.

1. The goalkeeper should start about 3 yards off his line, with the ball served by throwing it straight over his head from about 10 to 12 yards. The ball should have enough pace to prevent the goalkeeper from catching it.
2. Serve alternately, slightly to either side of the goalkeeper, but still over his head. Observe that the goalkeeper's choice of hand is correct for the situation.
3. Serve at random and observe the goalkeeper's technique.
4. Drop the ball and volley over the goalkeeper from 12 to 18 yards. Allow the goalkeeper to vary his distance from the goal-line.
5. Vary the service to include low shots, as well as some over the goalkeeper. Observe whether he adopts a position far enough out to save ordinary shots, whilst being able to get back quickly to turn the ball over the bar if it is played over him.
6. Observe the goalkeeper in match situations and return to the above practices as necessary.

B. DEFLECTING THE BALL ROUND THE POST

If the goalkeeper decides it is unsafe to try and hold a shot which is wide of him, he may elect to turn it round the post and out of play.

WHAT TO PRACTISE

In order to turn the ball round the post, he may need to reach up to four yards either side of him, that is, from the centre of the goal to the post. Given that when stretched most goalkeepers are 8 feet from fingers to feet, this will require a sideways leap of about 4 feet. Clearly, it is important that a goalkeeper is able to thrust off with considerable power. (This technique is covered in Section 6B, Part 1). Once the goalkeeper reaches the ball, it may be deflected with one or two hands. Two hands are preferable, as this gives a larger area to contact the ball, although for ground shots, one is often used. It is important that the palm of the hand is flat ,with fingers spread and a firm contact is made, so the direction of the ball is changed.

HOW TO PRACTISE

The organisation and progressions are the same as those for 6B above.

8. GETTING INTO LINE / NARROWING THE ANGLE.

So far, a whole range of techniques for stopping the ball have been dealt with, however, perhaps the most important single factor in goalkeeping is positioning. Unless the goalkeeper is in the correct position, he will either be unable to make a save at all, or the save will be much more difficult. Major aspects of positioning are 'getting into line' and 'narrowing the angle.' These give an attacker as small a target as possible.

WHAT TO PRACTISE.
A) GETTING INTO LINE.

As the ball changes position on the field, the goalkeeper should be continually changing his position also. This is achieved by small shuffling movements of the feet, keeping them close to the ground. At no time should the feet touch eachother or cross over and should be shoulder width apart to maintain good balance in readiness for a shot.

It is logical that with regard to shot stopping, a goalkeeper should be on the line from the ball to the centre of the goal, thus leaving gaps only at the corners of the goal. This is known as 'getting into line.'

B) STARTING POSITION FOR NARROWING THE ANGLE.

Once the goalkeeper has got into line from the centre of his goal to the ball, it is vital that he then 'narrows the angle', the question being, "where on that line should he be?" The answer to this depends on the position of the ball. When the ball is in the attacking third, the goalkeeper should be some 18 yards out. When the ball is in the middle third of the field, he should be 6 to 12 yards out. When the ball is in the defending third, he should be 4 to 6 yards out. The goalkeeper's exact position will depend on his personal preference and whether the ball is in a wide or central position. The more central the ball, the further out the goalkeeper is likely to be. In all these positions, he is well placed to make a save should a shot be taken. He will also have less distance to cover should he need to come out to a ball played behind the defence.

The goalkeeper is on the goal-line in the centre of the goal. The attacking player can see a large part of the goal to either side, thus making it easier for him to score. The goalkeeper must also move a long way to make a save.

The goalkeeper has come half of the way towards the attacking player, but not far enough, as the attacker can still score to either side of the goalkeeper fairly easily.

The goalkeeper has advanced far enough to greatly reduce the attacker's scoring chances with a direct shot. The goalkeeper will only have a small distance to move to make a save, however he will not have much time, therefore quick reactions are needed. The danger area now is behind the goalkeeper and he may be vulnerable to the ball being lobbed over or dribbled round him.

C) DEVELOPMENT OF NARROWING THE ANGLE.

The above starting positions are also necessary should an attacker get clear of the defence and be one versus one against the goalkeeper. In such a situation the goalkeeper should come out, but only when the ball is out of the attacker's playing distance. The goalkeeper should advance quickly, but in a controlled manner. If the goalkeeper is first to the ball, he should secure it, or if outside the penalty area, fly kick the ball as high and far as possible.

If the attacker reaches the ball and shapes to shoot, the goalkeeper should stop and assume the ready position. He should not dive or fall down, thus making up the attacker's mind for him. The longer the goalkeeper can hold up the attacker and force him wide, the more chance there is of defenders getting back to make a challenge.

Should the attacker play the ball forward again, the goalkeeper may also advance. By advancing in this manner the goalkeeper may be able to fall on the ball or block the attacker's shot. This should be done as the attacker looks down at the ball to line up his shot, by falling sideways in a long barrier position, with both hands reaching out towards the ball with forearms close together. The goalkeeper must not fall 'feet-first' as this will not cover the maximum area of the goal (see diagram below). If the ball is not held first time, the goalkeeper should re-gain his feet quickly and fall onto it to complete the save.

HOW TO PRACTISE.

1. In an area 30 yards by 20 yards with a full size goal, the server plays the ball on the ground into the shaded square for A1 to run onto. Initially, A1 is only allowed one touch. The goalkeeper may start wherever he chooses, up to 5 yards off his line. When A1 reaches the ball, observe how far the goalkeeper has advanced. This should be at least as far as the attacker. It should also be in a direct line from the centre of the goal to the ball. The goalkeeper's first move must therefore be 'into line' and will involve a sideways shuffling movement with feet shoulder width apart. The feet must never cross over.

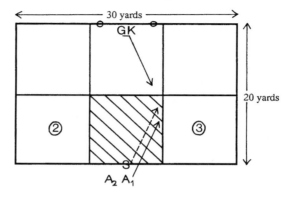

2. In addition to the distance and line of approach, observe that when A1 reaches the ball and draws his foot back to shoot, the goalkeeper has stopped advancing and has adopted the ready position.
3. Observe the goalkeeper's shot-stopping technique.
4. The ball may now be played on the ground into either of the squares 2 or 3 for A1 or A2. Both players should follow in for rebounds. Observe the goalkeeper as in 1 and 2 above.
5. The service may now include dropping and bouncing balls at random. Observe the position of the goalkeeper in relation to the ball being played over his head. The extent to which there is a possibility of this, will determine when and how far the goalkeeper should advance.
6. A1 and A2 may now shoot first time or take as many touches as they wish. Note all the goalkeeping techniques as above, but also his patience and ability to fall on the ball should A1 or A2 try to dribble round him. The more touches they have, the more the goalkeeper will have to re-adjust his position in relation to the ball and the centre of the goal. It is important that once the goalkeeper has advanced to narrow the angle, he should only retreat when the ball is played over him or when a defender has been able to position himself between the attacker and the goal-keeper. Similarly, if the point of attack is changed, the goalkeeper should move into, and down the new line of attack, as quickly as possible.

7. If the goalkeeper is satisfactory at narrowing the angle, but his blocking technique is poor, this may be coached in a 2 v 1 situation in a grid square.

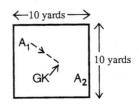

9. SPREADING.

WHAT TO PRACTISE.

Should an attacker try to dribble the ball around the goalkeeper, he will probably alter the angle/line of the ball. The goalkeeper should position himself on the new line of attack and if possible, fall on the ball. If it is played too wide for the goalkeeper to fall on, he will be required to spread himself as the attacker shoots, in order to cover as much of the goal as possible. This technique is similar to that for one versus one situations as in Section 8 above. When in doubt, the goalkeeper should stand up and not commit himself, thus forcing the attacker to make a decisive move.

As the attacker plays the ball past him, the goalkeeper covers the new line of attack and prepares to fall on the ball. Note the position of the hands.

The hands secure the ball, with one on top and one behind it. Note the sideways position of the body.

HOW TO PRACTISE.

As in narrowing the angle, but the attacker must initially try to dribble around the goalkeeper.

10. PUNCHING.

When high balls are played into the penalty area and the goalkeeper is under intense physical pressure, he may decide that it is too dangerous to catch the ball and instead elect to punch. The aim is to clear the ball from the immediate danger area with height and distance, although whether the ball will fall to a team-mate or an opponent is unpredictable.

WHAT TO PRACTISE.

When punching, two hands should be used whenever possible, as this gives a much larger area of contact. Both fists should be clenched and close together, the punch being achieved by straightening bent arms. Both hands should contact the ball simultaneously.

Before contact.
The arms are about to straighten to provide the force needed to clear the ball as far as possible. The backward-moving attacker would make attempting a catch risky.

HOW TO PRACTISE.

High balls may be served into the penalty area for the goalkeeper to catch or punch clear. A number of other players should put the goalkeeper under some pressure, although this should be carefully controlled. The goalkeeper should only be allowed to punch if it is unsafe to try and catch the ball.

11. DISTRIBUTION.

The goalkeeper is the one player who, in addition to kicking the ball, may choose to throw it. If he does kick it, he will use one of the techniques covered in the section on passing, most probably the lofted drive (for goal kicks), or the volley from the front (for kicks from the hands). The points for coaching kicking to goalkeepers are identical to those for other players and the same practices may be used, or goalkeepers may practise kicking techniques in pairs. Distribution should also be emphasised during all goalkeeping practices, with the ball being required to be returned accurately.

As a goalkeeper has a choice of kicking or throwing, what are the advantages of each? The major advantage of kicking is that great distance may be gained quickly. This is particularly useful when the opposition have been attacking and may not have a large number of players back in defensive positions. It may also be a good tactic if your team has one or two front players who are particularly strong in the air and who may create scoring chances from the ball being flicked on, or possession in an advanced position, from headers directed to team-mates. Normally, the target area for long kicks should be as shown in the diagram below. This is the area between the full backs' and centre backs' normal positions and may cause uncertainty in the opposition forcing them to attack the ball when moving sideways.

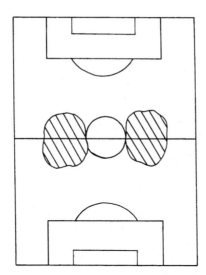

Where short kicks are taken, they should be played wide to minimise the risk of dangerous interceptions. It is recommended that they are only played to players who are in a position to easily play the ball forward. The main advantage of throwing is that usually a high degree of accuracy can be achieved, therefore there is a high degree of certainty that possession will be retained. The main argument for this is that without the ball, your team cannot score. The ball may be thrown for longer distances, but it is most used for 35 yards or less. It is normal for throws to be made to wide positions, where there is less danger from interceptions and from where forward play can be initiated easily.

WHAT TO PRACTISE.

There are three main techniques for throwing the ball.

A. ROLLING.

This technique is similar to ten pin bowling, the difference being that the ball rests in the open palm. The arm is straight and moves back in an arc, before coming forward and down, releasing the ball at the bottom of the arc and following through in the direction the ball has travelled. The feet are placed apart, one in front of the other, with the legs slightly bent. This technique can be used for distances up to 15 yards and has the advantage that it is easy to control, although it is also easy to read and lacks pace. The technique is simple and does not require intensive practice.

B. ONE-HANDED JAVELIN THROW.

As its name implies, this technique is similar to that of throwing the javelin. A sideways stance is taken, with the feet well apart and the ball resting in an open palm. The arm is bent and the ball thrown by bringing it forward at head height, with the fingers and thumb directing it. The hand should follow through in the direction of the throw. The non-throwing hand may be held forward to give balance. This technique is mainly used for distances of up to 25 yards and has the advantage that the ball can be thrown hard, although this may mean it is difficult to control, especially if bouncing. If the legs are bent during the throw this will help keep the trajectory of the ball low and therefore, it should be easier to control.

HOW TO PRACTISE.

1. Stand 15 yards away from the goalkeeper, who has a supply of footballs. Observe the technique as the goalkeeper throws. Return the balls to the goalkeeper and repeat.
2. As above, but signal alternately right or left, for the goalkeeper to throw slightly to that side. The ball should arrive without having bounced.
3. As above, but signal randomly right or left.
4. Increase the distance to 25 yards and repeat. Observe the technique and that the ball is reaching without bouncing.
5. Include two target players, one at 15 and one at 25 yards. The goalkeeper should throw to the correct player on the call of 'short' or 'long.' Observe how the goalkeeper adjusts to throwing different distances.
6. The receiving players should be encouraged to be moving forward as the goalkeeper prepares to throw.
7. As above, but a variety of balls are kicked to the goalkeeper by S1, who immediately runs to T1 or T2. The goalkeeper must secure the ball and throw immediately to the free player, who moves forward to receive the throw. Observe the technique. S1 changes place with whichever of T1 or T2 he has chosen to mark.

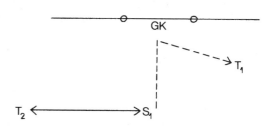

C. BOWLING OVER-ARM.

This is similar to the cricket bowling action and is a one-handed technique. A sideways stance is taken, with feet well apart. The front arm gives balance and points in the direction of the throw. The ball is held in an open hand and is trapped between the hand and lower arm until the moment of release. The arm comes upwards and over, with the moment of release being close to the arm's highest point, dependent on whether the ball is thrown upwards or downwards.

An upwards throw may be used for longer distances, or when there are opponents in the way. A downwards throw may be used when no opponent is in the way, as this will mean the ball will probably have stopped bouncing when it arrives and will be easier to control. This technique is mainly used for throws of 25 to 45 yards and has the advantage of being fast, when kept below head height. It is, however, easy to read and can be difficult to control.

Just before release. Note the weight coming forward onto the front leg and the eyes are watching the target.

HOW TO PRACTISE.

The organisation and progressions for this technique are identical to those in B above, except that the starting distance is 20 yards and this is later increased to 35 yards. For practice at throwing the ball over opponents, a player should be introduced to stand some 10-15 yards away from the goalkeeper, between him and the target.

CONCLUSION.

Over the years, coaching has come in for much criticism, principally from those who do not understand its intention or purpose. Stereotyped coaches will produce stereotyped players, but because coaching is very individualistic, with each of us having our own ideas and personality, this is bound to be reflected in our coaching. The intention of this book is not to produce stereotyped coaches or players, but to suggest principles of good practice, within which a coach should work, whilst developing his own ideas and opinions and encouraging his players to do the same.

Having read this book you should be in a much stronger position to set about coaching the techniques of Association Football. In addition to the basics of coaching - organisation, observation and communication - you should now be familiar with some of the coaching priorities and how to coach them. The reader is reminded, however, that no book of this length on such a complex subject can include every-thing, it can merely make you aware of the potential you have for making every player you coach, a better player. The rest is up to you!

INDEX

B

Ball control	41
basics of coaching	**8**
block tackle	79

C

Chipping the ball	35
choice of pass	16
coaching grids	9
coaching,the basics of	8
communication	11,14
control - cushion	41
wedge/firm	41
cushion control	43

D

Defending		**79**
	forcing play into certain areas	84
	preventing opponents playing forward	82
	preventing opponents turning	80
deflection heading		74
demonstrations		12,15
disguise		18
diving headers		77
dribbling		47
driving the ball		
	lofted	26
	low	24

F

Feedback	11
feinting	46
firm control	44
flick pass	33
forcing play into certain areas	84

G

Gaining time on the ball		**41**
	control	41
	dribbling	47
	feinting	46
	running with the ball	54
	turning	49
goalkeeping		**91**
	catching	93
	deflecting	100
	distribution	107
	diving	98
	getting into line	102
	ground techniques	97
	narrowing the angle	102
	punching	106
	ready position	92
	spreading	105
grids		9

H

Heading		**69**
	deflection	74
	diving	77
	in attack	72
	in defence	70
	introduction	69

I

Individual practice		8
instructions		
	demonstrations	12,15
	verbal instructions	11,14

K

Key factors	8

L

Lofted drive 26
low drive 24

O

Observation 10,14
organisation
    individual practices 8
    small-sided games 13

P

Pace of pass 20
pass selection 16
passing **16**
    qualities 16
    decisions 16
passing techniques 21
    chipping 35
    flick pass 33
    lofted drive 26
    low drive 24
    push pass 21
    volleying 37
preventing opponents playing
    forward 82
preventing opponents turning 80
progressive practice 7
push pass 21

R

Running with the ball 54

S

Secondary scoring chances 67
shooting **56**
    opportunities 63
    technique 61
    when not to shoot 57
    when to shoot 56
    where to shoot 58
small-sided games 12
swerving the ball 31

T

Tackling
    front block tackle 79
    side block tackle 79
    sliding tackle 79
technique 7
timing of a pass 18
turning with the ball 49

V

Verbal instructions 11,14
vision 19
volleying
    from the front 37
    from the side 38

W

Wedge control 44
weighting of a pass 20